Dedication

To my Mum – a proud, loveable woman. Now gone, but always remembered.
To my daughter Sharon, for being there when it got really tough.
To Kath, the dearest friend one could have.
To my husband Barry, for his patience and love.

Acknowledgments

Thanks to the many people who helped me along the way with this book.
Amongst them, my friend Jane Morgan for her encouragement and help;
Fay Winther, another friend, who made *NewStar on the Block* when I ran out of time,
and also allowed me to use a few more of her quilts made from my designs;
Nicole Bridges, Kaye Brown, Rhonda Coates and Kim Bradley for their long arm quilting expertise;
Mary Ellen Hopkins, just for being Mary Ellen and sharing her wonderful talent;
Kaye England, who taught me respect for traditional work, whilst encouraging me to push myself;
Bill Day from Dayview Fabrics for the commercial print fabric used in *Federation Medallion*;
Karen Fail, Megan Fisher and AQS for their support and confidence in me and other Australian authors;
and many others too numerous to list.
Without these people I could not have done it.

Contents

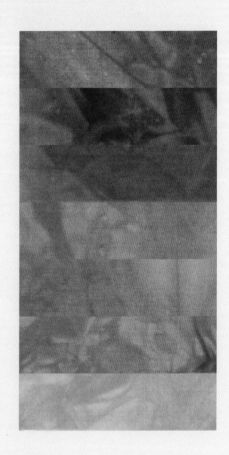

FABRIC
Fandango

Combining Hand Dyed and Commercial Prints

Gail Simpson

Fabric Fandango: combining hand dyed and commercial prints
By Gail Simpson

American Quilter's Society
P.O. Box 3290
Paducah, Kentucky 42002-3290

Located in Paducah, Kentucky, the American Quilter's Society (AQS) is dedicated to promoting the accomplishments of today's quilters. Through its publications and events, AQS strives to honor today's quiltmakers and their work and to inspire future creativity and innovation in quiltmaking.

Editors: Karen Fail and Megan Fisher
Design and Layout: Luba Bosch
Illustrations: Susan Cadzow of Red Pepper Graphics
Cover Design: Michael Buckingham
Photography: Photographix
Cover Quilt: Autumn Geese – designed by Gail Simpson; patchwork by Fay Winther, quilting by Rhonda Coates

Library of Congress Cataloging-in-Publication Data

Simpson, Gail.
  Fabric fandango : combining hand dyed and commercial prints / By Gail Simpson.
    p. cm.
  Summary: "Learn to combine graduated hand-dyed fabrics with commercial prints. Traditional and original quilt projects designed to showcase the mix of fabrics. Detailed cutting and sewing directions provided along with instructions on choosing the fabrics" --Provided by publisher.
  ISBN 978-1-57432-939-1
  1. Dyes and dyeing--Textile fibers. I. Title.

TT853.S95 2007
746.6--dc22
                2007019860

Additional copies of this book may be ordered from the American Quilter's Society,
PO Box 3290, Paducah, KY 42002-3290, or online at: www.AmericanQuilter.com.

Produced by:
QuiltWorks
Promoting Australian and New Zealand quiltmaking and quiltmakers
17 Peter Close
Hornsby Heights, NSW
AUSTRALIA 2077

Introduction

Nineteen years ago I moved from the city to a semi-rural area. I had been working for many years in the fields of computing and accounting and decided it was time to get back to the things I loved to do. At the top of the list was more sewing.

I took a couple of classes at a local patchwork shop and learned the basics, but was not quite hooked. I bought myself a rotary cutter, ruler and mat, some fabrics and a copy of Mary Ellen Hopkins' *The It's Okay If You Sit On My Quilt Book*. That book opened up a whole new world to me! The only problem was, I didn't get any 'vibes' from the print fabrics I could buy and there was not enough scope in the plain/solid fabrics that were available.

At the time I was working with dyeing silks, and the light came on: dye cottons! To cut a long story short, a visitor asked if he could take my fabrics and try to sell them. From that point on, I was a fabric wholesaler. Who in their right mind would start a labor intensive business when approaching 50?

For the first few years, I was selling sets of light, medium and dark fabrics by the metre, with a range of about fifty colors. I was also making the occasional quilt to help promote my fabrics.

I attended workshops with Mary Ellen Hopkins and realized that I spent too much time choosing fabrics for my quilts. The concept of a pack of hand dyed fabrics in sets of ten or twelve coordinating colors was born; all I needed to add to make a quilt were one or two commercial prints. At first I found this approach restrictive; however the more I worked with the concept the easier it became. In this book I share some of what I have learned.

The biggest influence in my quiltmaking in the past five or so years has been Kaye England. She taught me to respect traditional work and the eye opening use of specialty rulers.

As a result, I have challenged myself to work on more traditionally styled quilts with a contemporary influence and design quilts incorporating the various techniques I have learned and developed along the way.

For the past four years, I have also been known as the 'Pfaff Floozy', due to my association with Pfaff here in Australia as an Ambassador for Pfaff sewing machines. As a result, I have been able to enter the world of machine embroidery and have seen the impact of computerized embroidery in quilting explode in the last few years. I have used machine embroidery in several of the quilts in this book; I am most proud of the simple design I digitized myself for *Gretchen's Makeover*.

When designing quilts, my objectives for each and every quilt (in addition to showcasing my fabrics), are to:
• include something to learn
• include a technique or design element that can be expanded on
• allow for input from the maker to put their own stamp on the work
• allow for the original design to have a place to grow.

I have implemented this approach with the quilts in this book, and list below the specific focus of each of them.

Almost Country	A simple block developed to showcase a color range
Autumn Geese	Directional designing and working the grid
Birds and Bouquet Fantasy	Loved the Migrating Geese and needed to use the technique
Candy Canes	Working with a diagonal print
Fandango	Paper piecing or templates
Federation Medallion	A display for my favorite color set and a little bit of embroidery
For the Print	Mixing straight cuts and curves – and a place to use that precious commercial print
Fun with Nine-patch	A fun technique with lots of room for embroidery, quilting and/or appliqué
Gretchen's Makeover	The block I never wanted to make – until I saw the Kaye England way!
Kites Afloat	Floating the traditional kaleidoscope design
NewStar on the Block	Two great techniques
Not Quite 1000 Pyramids	Using a ruler as a template and a good reason for peeper strips
RailStar	Designing on a grid
Topsy Turvy	Getting started with quick cutting and piecing techniques

Many of the quilts provide room to grow. *Almost Country*, for example, could be turned on point and become a great center medallion for a larger quilt. Alternatively, think smaller: *Not Quite 1000 Pyramids* makes a great cot quilt when made with smaller units and a pretty commercial print.

All the projects in this book have step-by-step directions and if you are new to the world of quiltmaking, I would encourage you to read the Quilting Basics section before beginning a project. I also suggest you start with one of the easier projects, say *Topsy Turvy*. If you are looking for more of a challenge, why not tackle *NewStar on the Block*? I have added a rating to each set of instructions so that you can see before you begin whether it's within your current capabilities or is a challenge that will help you to grow them further.

The Gallery pages showcase more quilts that combine hand dyed and commercial print fabrics. I hope you are inspired, delighted and eager to start on your own creations.

How to combine hand dyed and commercial print fabrics

WHY USE HAND DYED FABRICS?

Hand dyed fabrics offer quiltmakers an array of options that aren't necessarily available from commercial print fabrics.

- First and foremost, hand dyed fabrics come in almost every color of the rainbow. Whilst that might be true, in theory, of plain/solid quilter's fabrics, not many quilt shops stock a large selection of them. You might find half a dozen or, if it's a large store, perhaps a dozen shades of blue, for example. But not quite the shade that you're after, or not the gentle gradations of color that you need to add the 'wow' factor to your quilt or the subtlety of shades that will combine to create just the mood you're looking for. Hand dyed fabrics, in contrast, are often sold in packs of gradated colors, with a wide selection available. That means that for a fairly modest cost, you can leave the store with 10 shades of blue and 15 shades of red, along with a dozen purples that join the two in a gorgeous color progression. Having such a palette of color opens the door to all sorts of possibilities.

- Many hand dyed fabrics also feature subtle texture, making them more interesting to the eye than plain/solid fabrics. As quiltmakers who enjoy intricate appliqué will attest, this slightly inconsistent uptake of the dye provides wonderful opportunities to create realistic shadings in fruit, flowers and everything in between. Hand dyed fabrics are also excellent choices for the background of appliqué blocks, being less stark than solid colors without the distraction of commercial prints. The texture of hand dyed fabrics is a boon for patchworkers too. It adds understated complexity to a quilt with absolutely no greater effort

Hand dyed fabrics are often available in gradated colors

than working with plain/solid fabrics. When the patches in a block are clearly the same color, but ever so slightly different, the eye is intrigued – sometimes without even knowing quite why.

- Another benefit of using hand dyed fabrics in patchwork blocks is that both sides of the fabric are of equal quality: there's no right side or wrong side. This means that quiltmakers don't need to fuss with cutting shapes in reverse for those designs that feature mirror-imaged shapes. My personal preference is for designing and making geometric-design patchwork quilts, and the need to mirror-reverse cuts arises frequently. However, when I'm using hand dyed fabrics, the problem simply disappears! Cutting fabric for *Not Quite 1000 Pyramids* (page 33) and *Fandango* (page 72), for example, is much more straightforward when reversing templates is made unnecessary. All the shapes are cut the same way, then some are just flipped over to the 'wrong' side.

There is no need to cut around templates in reverse when working with hand dyed fabrics.

- Using hand dyed fabrics enables even a beginner quiltmaker to create a one-of-a-kind quilt. No one else will have exactly the same fabric, so even if a whole workshop class is working on the same quilt design and everyone is using hand dyed fabrics, each and every quilt will still be unique.

HOW CAN I USE HAND DYED FABRICS IN MY QUILTS?

Quiltmakers have been using hand dyed fabrics in their quilts for decades. It seems, however, that many quiltmakers believe that hand dyed fabrics are only suitable for Baltimore Album-style appliqué or, at the other end of the continuum, cutting edge art quilts, but not much in between.

I admit that one of my first exposures to hand dyed fabrics in quiltmaking was in the works of

Caryl Bryer Fallert. Many readers will recognize Caryl's name, and associate it with a brave and wonderful use of saturated color. It's also true to say, however, that many readers will categorize Caryl's work as avant garde art quiltmaking, featuring, as it does, twisted tucks, one-off designs and, in more recent times, images scanned and manipulated by computer. Along the way, Caryl's use of hand dyed and painted fabrics has been inextricably linked with the style of quilt that she makes. And thus, in many minds, hand dyed fabrics have been perceived as being suitable only for that kind of quilt.

Quiltmakers who adore traditional appliqué designs are also long-standing devotees of hand dyed fabrics. Such famous names as Elly Sienkiewicz and Nancy Pearson have advocated the use of hand dyed fabrics for adding realism to leaves, flower petals and the like; indeed, Elly has suggested that hand dyed fabrics effectively imitate the shaded rainbow fabrics that are one of the identifying characteristics of a classic Baltimore Album quilt. Shop owners seem to endorse this use of hand dyed fabrics by stocking packs of fabrics in small-ish cuts and charm squares.

My quilts fall into neither of these camps. I began with traditional patchwork blocks, and over the years have explored a variety of techniques to make their creation faster, more accurate, more fun and more innovative. I have also dabbled in appliqué, although it's not my first love. When I do appliqué, I like large-ish, simple shapes that are often funky and fun rather than petite and pastel.

My key objective in writing *Fabric Fandango* is to provide you with evidence that hand dyed fabrics work perfectly well, wonderfully well in patchwork quilts that are clearly based in traditional designs. The hand dyed fabrics can be the feature of the quilt, or they can play a supporting role, allowing the commercial print to star.

If you want to make a traditional-looking quilt, think about what makes the patchwork design effective; it's often value rather than color. That means that you'll need to ensure that you purchase hand dyed fabrics of light, medium and dark values. This is exactly the same 'trick' that you need to apply if you were making the quilt entirely from commercial print fabrics.

Left to my own devices, most of my quilts would be bright, bright, bright, showcasing hand dyed fabrics, and using commercial prints as backdrops. But as a quilt designer and teacher, I am often called upon to design and make quilts that appeal to others. Soft pastel hand dyed fabrics can be simply gorgeous. See the light sections in *Fandango* for example. And although I've used quite bright hand dyed fabrics in *Federation Medallion* and *Birds and Bouquet Fantasy,* it's easy to imagine that softer shades would have been equally successful.

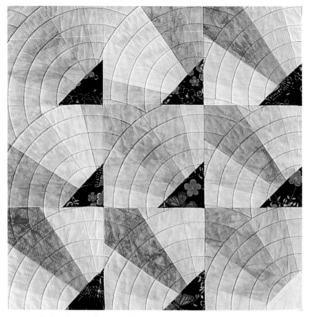

Hand dyed pastels were featured in Fandango *(see page 72).*

I know from my experience as a wholesaler of hand dyed fabrics that the pastel shades outsell the brighter ones. That seems to me to be as good an indication as any that there are quiltmakers using these softer colors to make masterpieces. They are extremely popular for babies' quilts and, I suspect, for appliqué backgrounds.

Hand dyed fabrics are also popular for use in landscape and pictorial quilts. Several years ago I introduced a new assortment of hand dyed fabrics into my range entitled 'Leaf and Litter', using the colors of the leaf litter on a forest floor. It quickly moved close to the top of the sales charts, bested only by pastels.

I'm hoping that *Fabric Fandango* will result in more quiltmakers experimenting with hand dyed fabrics across the color and value spectrum, choosing hand dyed fabrics for all manner of uses in all manner of quilts.

Hand dyed fabrics are popular choices for landscape quilts and baby quilts.

HOW SHOULD I COMBINE HAND DYED FABRICS WITH COMMERCIAL PRINTS?

There are many answers to this question; I guess my short answer is that you should combine hand dyed fabrics with commercial prints in any manner that pleases you. Forget the Quilt Police; if you like what you're creating, that's what matters most of all. In *Fabric Fandango* however, I'll show you a method that I've been using with success for many years.

I've had the good fortune to have attended workshops with some of the world's leading quiltmakers. I've learned a lot from Mary Ellen Hopkins' books and from being a student in a number of her classes. Of all the things that I learned at those workshops, the one that has had the greatest impact on my quiltmaking is that I was spending far too long choosing colors and fabrics for my quilts.

Like many quiltmakers, I have had no formal education in color or art; when I began making quilts, I lacked confidence in my ability to choose fabrics that would work well together.

As I became more involved in dyeing my own fabrics, my knowledge and understanding of color grew – but I was still agonizing over choices for any particular quilt project. I decided to make the task easier by limiting myself to only one or two commercial prints per quilt and whatever hand dyed fabrics coordinated with them. At first this self-imposed restriction was difficult, but I stuck with it, and over time, it became not only easier but also stimulating and successful. I didn't feel the need to spend so much time struggling with fabric choices: I could dive into actually making quilts.

All the quilts in this book are examples of adopting this successful 'formula'. It's certainly not the only way of combining hand dyed fabrics and commercial prints, but it does make choosing fabrics a whole lot easier. It's especially easy if you buy a coordinated pack of hand dyed fabrics. Most hand dyers

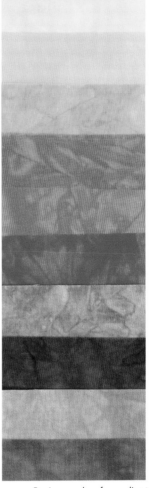

Buying packs of coordinated hand dyed fabrics makes choosing fabrics easy.

sell their wares in this manner, so you can see the array in a pack, determine if you like it, and if you do, much of the challenge of choosing colors for your next project has been done for you. With only one or two commercial print fabrics to select as accompaniments, you're almost there.

Of course, there's nothing to stop you from increasing the number of commercial print fabrics that you use in your quilt; it's just that I have found this approach so liberating and stimulating, that I'd encourage you to experiment with it.

HOW SHOULD I CHOOSE HAND DYED FABRICS?

Color, color and color are the three most important considerations! Beyond that, however, you do need to consider quality. Just as there are

In Topsy Turvy (page 13), hand dyed fabrics are combined with just one commercial print fabric.

different qualities of commercial print fabrics, so there are different qualities of hand dyed fabrics.

One key consideration in determining quality is the nature of the base cloth. Many hand dyed fabrics shrink as they're being processed, making them thicker and bulkier. If at all possible, arrange to handle the hand dyed fabrics that you are going to purchase to gauge their density, weave, and drape.

Another key consideration is colorfastness. These days, it is quite possible to hand dye cotton fabrics in a manner that ensures that they are at least as colorfast as commercial prints. Ask your dyer what processes have been used, whether you need to pre-wash the fabric prior to using it in your quilts, and what assurances you can be given about dye bleeding from the fabric.

If you imagine that you will be buying fabric over time and want it to match, or if you are buying multiple small cuts of one shade of hand dyed fabric, you may also want to give some consideration to color matching. Many hand dyers pride themselves on the uniqueness of each and every length of fabric that they dye. Even though they may use standard recipes to achieve certain colors, they do not aim to achieve uniformity between batches. What's more, variations in the dye powders that hand dyers use – even when they are buying exactly the same powder from the same manufacturer – make it impossible for them to guarantee exact matches between dye lots.

That means that if you've underpurchased a particular shade and need to buy some more three months later when you've decided to use it in the borders, you may find that the fabric that you buy, even though it's from the same supplier and has the same name, is not quite the same color. Often times this won't matter, but there will be occasions when it's important.

Choose one feature print to combine with hand dyeds, and let the fabric do the work.

WHAT KINDS OF COMMERCIAL PRINTS WORK WELL WITH HAND DYED FABRICS?

I'll start with what I think doesn't work terribly well. To my mind, there's little point combining hand dyed fabrics with tone-on-tone commercial prints or mottled prints. They only serve to devalue your treasured hand dyed fabrics.

Other than that, virtually any and every commercial print is a candidate for being combined successfully with hand dyed fabrics. If you love the look of antique quilts, work with muted shades of hand dyed fabrics and some of the reproduction prints now readily available.

If you're more interested in bright quilts, stripes, dots, batiks and novelty prints all look marvelous along side hand dyed fabrics. Then there are those I refer to as 'accent' or 'feature' prints. The turkey feather print in *Almost Country* and the glorious bird print in *Birds and Bouquet Fantasy* are good examples of these.

Hand dyed fabrics work well with reproduction commercial prints.

There seems to be a stereotype that many quilters share: that hand dyed fabrics work best with black background fabrics. Certainly hand dyed fabrics are widely used in stained glass patchwork and they look stunning. But that's not to suggest that that is the only kind of background fabric that can be used.

Because I tend towards stronger, brighter colors in my quilts, I do often reach for a dark commercial print to accompany the hand dyed fabrics. But I rarely use just a plain black. Look at *Topsy Turvy* for example: a deep dark blue and black commercial print adds much more visual interest and character to the quilt than a plain black would have done.

Another 'trick' to enhancing the look of your quilts is to use dark commercial prints that have some movement in their design. The background fabric in *RailStar*, for example, combines swirls of deep purple and green on a dark background, with extra movement stemming from the black reeds printed over the top of the colors. (I do wish I had not limited myself to purchasing only three metres of this one!)

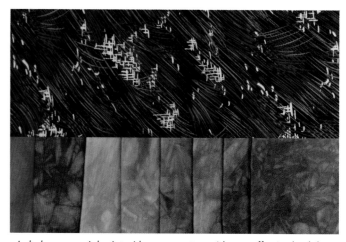

A dark commercial print with movement provides an effective backdrop for a set of hand dyed fabrics.

I did use plain black in *Gretchen's Makeover* I must admit. But in that case, I wanted to feature machine embroidery, and I felt that a solid black background would ensure that there was nothing to distract the eye from the stitching.

Light backgrounds are another story. I have found that those that work very well have a pale background with little specks of color dotted here, there and everywhere. Those little specks of color lead to the selection of the hand dyed colors. From time to time I do dye light fabrics, mixing up left over dyes, with the intention of using them as background fabrics in a quilt. In most instances where I use these, they could be replaced with these 'speckled' commercial print fabrics.

Another successful light fabric – found in the 'sale' bin at a local quilting shop – is the soft grey print used in *Kimono Trio* (shown in the Gallery). Yes I bought the lot! Soft greys like this are great with hand dyed fabrics. They work more effectively than tone-on-tone beige or white commercial print fabrics: white is generally too stark and in my experience, a beige needs to be exactly the right shade if it is not to compete with yellow hand dyed fabrics.

Soft greys such as this one usually combine effectively with hand dyed fabrics.

Don't be afraid to choose commercial prints with visual interest as background fabrics.

My personal thoughts on fabrics to be used as backgrounds, be they light or dark: the plainer they are, the more quilting required. Because I don't enjoy quilting by hand and I am not an expert machine quilter – my joy is in dyeing fabrics, designing original quilts and patchworking – I tend to choose commercial print fabrics for my backgrounds that have a bit of pizzazz and visual interest and aren't just a place to feature the quilting stitches.

SHOULD I CHOOSE THE COMMERCIAL PRINT OR THE HAND DYED FABRICS FIRST?

Either approach will work. The approach to use in any given situation, however, depends on your objective.

If you see a commercial print fabric that you can't live without, buy it. There are so many

shades of hand dyed fabrics available that you can be confident of being able to find those that will combine with your precious fabric perfectly.

This is what happened to me when I created *For the Print*. I saw the large Alexander Henry print in a quilt shop; I had no idea what I would use it for, but it just picked me up and shook me and I knew that I wanted to use it in a quilt. I put off cutting into that print for more than 20 months, and then was only able to do so after I'd designed a quilt that enabled me to keep large sections of the fabric intact. I dyed dark, medium and light shades of blue ash, red and grey to use in the project, although I didn't end up using all nine fabrics. In the end, I felt that such an array would have distracted from the print, so I limited my selection.

I adopted the same approach for *Fun with Nine-patch*, which features a fabulous commercial print with many colors. I chose only two colors from the print for my hand dyeds – scarlet and ochre – and set the blocks in a light background. Simplicity of design, strong clean lines and open style circular embroidery was all the 'wow' the print needed. A red colorway of the same commercial print fabric is used in *Scarlet*, one of the quilts in the Gallery, and again it is paired with only two hand dyed fabrics.

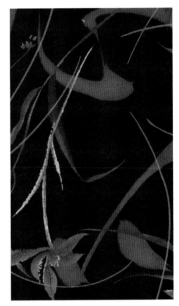

A precious commercial print that became the starting point for For the Print.

Generally speaking, when I see a commercial print fabric that appeals very strongly to me, I buy two or three yards, and then set about picking hand dyed fabrics to use with it. I imagine that many of those large Japanese prints would look stunning with hand dyed fabrics – although again, the challenge would be to use the hand dyed fabrics in supporting roles only, not allowing them to overwhelm the commercial print.

Equally, it's quite feasible to buy a pack of hand dyed fabrics, and then take it to a quilt shop to find a commercial print that works well with it. When you work in this manner, I recommend that you start by simply choosing an array of hand dyed fabrics that you like and would be happy to work with. Cut a smidgen from each

Two colorways of the same commercial print fabric demonstrate how readily hand dyed fabrics can be found that will combine well with almost any print you fall in love with.

fabric to make a sample card. Keep it in your handbag so that whenever you happen to be in a quilt shop, you can refer to it.

It's not important to find a commercial print that has every color of your sample card in it. Indeed, if you task yourself to do this, you may be looking for years for the 'perfect' commercial print. Instead, look for a print that has a 'wow' factor for you and includes two or three of the hand dyed fabric colors in it.

Start with a gorgeous array of hand dyed fabrics, then find a commercial print to work with them.

Kimono Trio is a good example. The commercial print fabric I used in those projects features peachy apricot and dusty blue butterflies. I chose it to complement the fabrics in my Mellows 2 pack of hand dyeds.

When you start with a pack of hand dyed fabrics, the commercial prints you choose don't need to have every color in them.

Now, not all of the colors included in Mellows 2 are found in the commercial print, but those that aren't, still work well with those that are. So, to a large extent, it's true to say that if you have a range of hand dyed fabrics that look good together, then you can be fairly confident of combining them in a quilt with a commercial print fabric that has at least some of them in it. What's more the colors that aren't present in the commercial print can be inspired choices as accent colors in your finished quilt.

If you are new to hand dyed fabrics, I recommend that you start by purchasing a color coordinated pack of hand dyeds, then seek out commercial print(s). When conducting workshops in a quilting shop, I actually go through this exercise with the students, encouraging them to step outside their

Strips work surprisingly well with hand dyed fabrics.

comfort zone and view the commercial prints as supporting fabrics for their first choice – the pack of hand dyed fabrics they couldn't live without!

Another suggestion is to pair your pack of hand dyed fabrics with a pack of fat eighths from a fabric range that appeals to you. Choose a background that will work with both the hand dyed fabrics and the commercial print fabrics and make a sampler style quilt using various blocks and techniques in the projects.

LET'S START MAKING QUILTS!

All the projects in this book are rated for beginner, intermediate or advanced patchworkers. Choose a project that fits your ability and a color scheme that suits you.

Don't be limited by the color choices that I have made. *Federation Medallion* can become *Summer Star* simply by changing the color scheme using colors such as those in the Cotton Patch Fabrics' Summer Medley pack.

My original version of *Topsy Turvy* was made using a pack of hand dyed fabrics that I call 'Shadows' and a tan print with a few wavy lines of red and blue, making it a great quilt for a young male friend.

The cover quilt – *Autumn Geese* – was originally made as *Summer Geese* with hand dyed fabrics in blues, greens and yellows and a wonderful swirly commercial print fabric suggesting the sea and summer.

Be brave. To use a typically Australian expression: take a punt and have a go!

Leftover hand dyed fabrics are never a problem – there is always a project where you can use them. How about using them to make a scrappy version of a traditional patchwork quilt, for example? In lieu of the variation in value that many such quilts rely on, try working with the variation commercial print/hand dyed. Every time you finish a project, cut a few patches of the leftover hand dyed fabrics and keep them in a box (with your template or rotary cutting instructions – so you remember what size to cut). When you have enough variety, make some blocks for your scrappy quilt.

They are also great for plate blades – just see what I did with them in *In a Spin* and *Triple the Fun* in the Gallery section.

You will also find in the Gallery several other examples of quilts that I have designed that combine hand dyed and commercial print fabrics. Perhaps you could call them Brain Food for Patchworkers!

Happy stitching.

Topsy Turvy

Designed and made by Gail Simpson; quilted by Nicole Bridges
Finished size: 59½in x 69½in (151cm x 176.5cm)
Finished block size: 5in square

Topsy Turvy

THIS QUILT IS MADE WITH A VARIATION on the basket weave block. The center sections of the blocks are strip-pieced wedges, made in a long strip and then cut to size. The hand dyed colors are mixed at random, with no rhyme or reason. The quilt is made of hand dyed fabrics in ten different colors, but you could use a few more or a few less if you wished.

MATERIALS

⅜yd (30cm) each of 10 different colored hand dyed fabrics. Gail used medium values of daffodil, golden yellow, peach, orange, pink, red violet, purple, agapanthus, blue and green.

3¼yd (2.9m) dark blue mottled commercial print fabric. This is sufficient for the quilt only. You will need to buy extra if you wish to make the matching cushion. Refer to the Materials list for the cushion on page 17.

3⅝yd (3.3m) backing fabric

64in x 74in (161cm x 187cm) batting

Post-it notes or small sticky labels

Neutral thread for piecing

Rotary cutter, mat and ruler

Sewing machine

General sewing supplies

CUT THE FABRIC

1. From the dark blue mottled commercial print fabric, cut:
- 30 strips, 1½in x width of fabric (blocks)
- 5 strips, 5½in x width of fabric (Border 1). See the tip in 'Make the blocks' before cutting these strips.
- 7 strips, 2½in x width of fabric (Border 3)
- 7 strips, 2¼in x width of fabric (binding)

2. Press each length of hand dyed fabric and stack them on top of each other, raw edges matching. Trim the selvage at one short end. Measure 32in from this cut edge and cut through all the layers. See Diagram 1. The surplus pieces will not be used in this project. Gail finds that she can cut quite accurately through ten layers of fabric at once using a large rotary cutter with a really shape blade in it. As an alternative, you could make two stacks of fabric, each with five fabrics in them and make the cuts.

32in

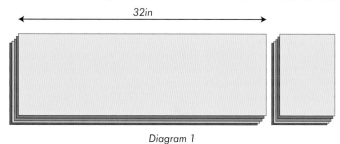

Diagram 1

3. Make 12 cuts across the 32in lengths of fabric in the stack, dividing them into 13 wedges. See Diagram 2. The wedges can be cut by eye: the narrow ends should be

Easy

between 1¼in and 1¾in and the wider ends between 2¾in and 3½in. If you are cutting your fabrics in two stacks each with five layers of fabric, you will need to ensure that the cuts are made in precisely the same places in each stack. An easy way to do this is to cut the first stack, then carefully lift the top layer of wedges from it and place them on top of the second stack. Use them as templates to guide the cutting of the second stack.

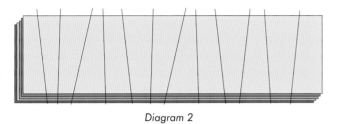

Diagram 2

4. Wedge stack #1 remains unchanged. For wedge stack #2, take the top layer of fabric and place it on the bottom of that stack. For wedge stack #3, take the top two layers of fabric and place them on the bottom. Continue in this manner, moving the top three layers of wedge stack #4, the top four layers of wedge stack #5, and so on until you have worked your way through all 13 stacks. See Diagram 3. When you have finished, there will be ten different colored wedges on the top layer: wedges 1 – 10 will each be different, and wedges 11 – 13 will repeat the first three colors. Use a Post-it note or sticky label to number each stack of wedges.

Diagram 3

MAKE THE BLOCKS

1. 111 are blocks required for this quilt, however they are very easy to make. Chain piecing is the most efficient way to work. Take wedge stacks #1 and #2 to your sewing machine. Flip the wedge on the top of stack #2 over on to the wedge on the top of stack #1, so the two wedges are right side together. Offset wedge #2 a little, and stitch the two wedges together. See Diagram 4.

2. Repeat with the second layer of wedges in each stack, then the third, and so on in one long chain.

3. Take the complete chain of wedge pairs to the ironing board. Start with the last pair of wedges you sewed together. Cut them loose from the chain, flip wedge #2 over so that its right side is facing up and press. Repeat with each pair of wedges, taking care to keep them in order, and stacking them on top of each other after they are pressed. The last pair will have your sticky labels on them.

Diagram 4

4. Repeat steps 1–3 to sew wedges #3 and #4 together in pairs. Work through all the stacks, sewing wedges #5 and #6 together, #7 and #8 together, and so on. The wedges in stack #13 will remain unsewn at this stage. Press all the seams in the same direction as you work.

5. The next step is to chain piece pairs of wedges together. Repeat steps 1–3 with the stack of 1+2 wedges and the stack of 3+4 wedges. Sew the pairs of wedges in these stacks together, taking care to keep them in order. Cut them apart, press them, and restack them in the correct order. Repeat with other pairs of wedge stacks.

6. Next sew stacks of four wedges to each other. Then sew strips of wedges 1–8 to the strips of wedges 9–12 to create 10 strips of 12 wedges. Finally, add wedge #13 to the end of each strip. Remove the labels from the top layer of wedges.

7. Each strip of 13 wedges will measure about 26in long. Trim one of the long edges of each strip. Cross cut each strip into three narrower strips 3½in wide. See Diagram 5.

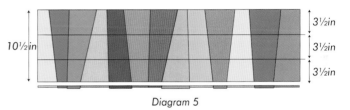

Diagram 5

8. Sew a 1½in strip of dark blue mottled commercial print fabric to each long edge of the narrow strips. The strips should now be 5½in wide from raw edge to raw edge. Refer to the tip below. Cross cut the strips into 5½in squares. See Diagram 6. You will need 111 blocks in total.

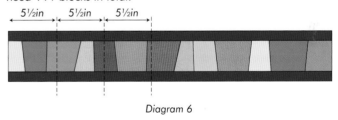

Diagram 6

Tip

If your strips aren't precisely 5½in wide, that is fine; what's important is that all your strips are the same width. Measure your strips and if they are not 5½in, substitute your measurement to cut the squares in step 8. And in the following instructions for the borders, wherever the 5½in width is mentioned, use your measurement instead.

9. Lay out the blocks in nine rows of seven blocks each. (You will have lots of blocks left over.) In the odd numbered rows, begin and end with the dark blue mottled strips in the block lying vertically. In the even numbered rows, begin and end with the dark blue strips in the block lying horizontally. Mix and match the blocks until you have an array of colors that you find appealing.

10. Join the blocks in each row together. Then join the rows together, carefully matching seams.

ADD BORDER 1

1. Referring to Adding Borders in Quilting Basics, page 89, join the five 5½in strips of dark blue mottled commercial print fabric end to end. Measure the width of the quilt. Trim two strips this length from the long strip. Put them aside.

2. Measure the length of the quilt. Trim two strips this length from the remainder of the long strip. Sew them to the left and right edges of the quilt. Press seams towards the border strips.

3. Stitch a block to each end of the border strips cut in step 1; orientate the blocks so that the dark blue mottled strips in each block lie horizontally. Sew these strips to the top and bottom edges of the quilt, matching seams. Refer to the Quilt Layout Diagram as you work.

ADD BORDER 2

1. Lay out two rows of 11 blocks each. In each row, begin and end with the dark blue mottled strips in the block lying horizontally. Mix and match the blocks until you have an array of colors that you like. Join the blocks in each row together.

2. Join these rows of blocks to the left and right edges of the quilt. (The dark blue mottled strips in the first block in each strip will now lie vertically in the quilt.) Press the seams towards Border 1.

3. Lay out another two rows of 11 blocks each. In each row, begin and end with the dark blue mottled strips in the block lying horizontally. Join the blocks in each row together, then join the rows to the top and bottom edges of the quilt. Press the seams towards Border 1.

ADD BORDER 3

1. Join the seven 2½in strips of dark blue mottled fabric end to end to make one long strip.

2. Referring to Adding Borders in Quilting Basics, page 89, measure the length of the quilt. Trim two strips this length from the long strip. Sew them to the left and right edges of the quilt.

3. Measure the width of the quilt. Trim two strips this length from the remainder of the long strip. Sew them to the top and bottom edges of the quilt.

FINISH THE QUILT

1. Cut the length of backing fabric in half. Remove the selvages. Referring to Piecing the Backing in Quilting Basics, page 89, join the two sections and trim to 52in x 65in for the backing of the quilt.

2. Referring to Preparing the Quilt Sandwich in Quilting Basics, page 89, layer the backing, batting and quilt ready for quilting.

3. Quilt as desired. *Topsy Turvy* was machine quilted by Nicole Bridges. She worked an edge to edge pattern on her long arm machine using multicolored thread.

4. Join the seven strips cut for the binding end to end to make one long strip. Use it to bind the quilt, referring to Binding the Quilt in Quilting Basics, page 89.

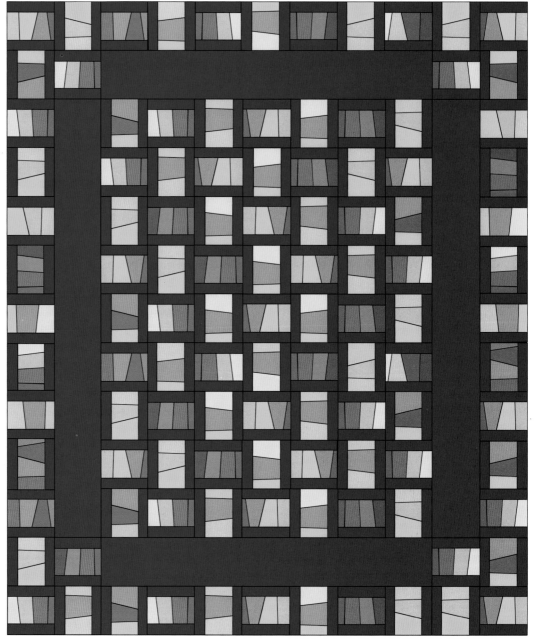

Quilt Layout Diagram

Topsy Turvy Cushion

THE SURPLUS BLOCKS left over after completing the Topsy Turvy quilt can be used to make a matching cushion.

MATERIALS

Surplus blocks left from *Topsy Turvy* quilt
⅝yd (60cm) dark blue mottled commercial print fabric
Thin batting at least 26in (65cm) square
Size 20 (20in/50cm) square cushion form
Thread to match the dark blue fabric
Rotary cutter, mat and ruler
Sewing machine
General sewing supplies

MAKE THE CUSHION FRONT

1. From the dark blue mottled commercial print fabric, cut:
• One strip, 7½in x width of fabric. Cross cut two squares, 7½in. Cut each square once on the diagonal to yield four half-square triangles (corners).
Trim the remainder of the strip to 7in, and from it cross cut two squares, 7in. Cut each square twice on the diagonals to yield a total of eight quarter-square triangles (setting triangles).

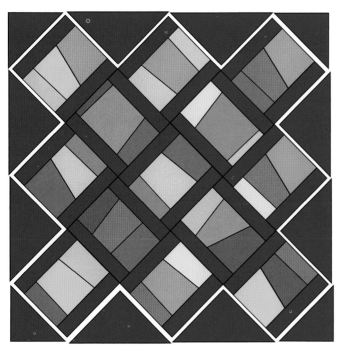

Cushion Layout Diagram

• One strip 12in x width of fabric. Cross cut it into two rectangles, 12in x 21½in (cushion back).
2. Lay out 13 of the blocks left over from the *Topsy Turvy* quilt, referring to the Cushion Layout Diagram. Mix and match the blocks until you have an array of colors that you find appealing. Check that you have them orientated correctly. Add the setting and corner triangles of dark blue mottled print fabric to the layout.
3. Join the blocks and triangles in each diagonal row together, referring to Diagonal Setting in Quilting Basics, on page 89. Then join the rows together, carefully matching seams.
4. Trim the edges of the cushion to yield a square, 21½in.

FINISH THE CUSHION

1. Pin the cushion top to a square of batting.
2. Quilt as desired. *Topsy Turvy Cushion* was free machine quilted by Gail.
3. On one of the dark blue mottled rectangles for the cushion back, turn under a ¼in hem on one long edge. Turn it under again to make a double hem and stitch in place using thread to match the fabric.
4. Lay the cushion top right side up on a table. Place the unhemmed dark blue rectangle on top of it, right side down, and three edges aligned with the cushion top. Place the hemmed dark blue rectangle on the other end of the cushion, right side down, with the hemmed edge towards the center of the cushion. The two dark blue rectangles will overlap in the middle. Pin to hold the layers together.
5. Stitch around all four sides using a ½in seam.
6. Turn the cushion right side out through the opening in the back. Insert the cushion form.

Autumn Geese

A SINGLE PRINT to reflect the mood of the season, combined with a pack of ten hand dyed colors and two subtle commercial prints for backgrounds, and you have all the materials to make this easily pieced quilt. This method of constructing Flying Geese blocks was originally published by Mary Ellen Hopkins.

MATERIALS

12 hand dyed fat eighths [9in x 21in (25cm x 55cm)] in autumn tones (blocks and Border 1)

1yd (90cm) commercial print fabric in autumn tones (blocks and Border 2)

1⅝yd (1.5m) dark commercial print fabric (blocks and Border 1). You could choose a dark hand dyed fabric instead if you wished.

½yd (40cm) light commercial print fabric (blocks). You could choose a light hand dyed fabric instead if you wished.

3yd (2.8m) backing fabric

Batting at least 56in (142cm) square

Neutral thread for piecing

Rotary cutter, ruler and mat

Sewing machine and general sewing supplies

CUT THE FABRIC

Note: Before cutting the hand dyed fabrics, you must first decide on your color layout. Referring to the quilt photo, note that **six** colors are used in the center round of Flying Geese and **five** colors in the second round. All **12** colors are used in the squares for Border 1. Before you begin to cut, separate your colors into two sets, one for each round of Flying Geese. One hand dyed fabric won't be used at all for the Flying Geese – it is only used in Border 1.

From each of the six hand dyed fabrics you've chosen for the center round, cut:
• Four rectangles, 2½in x 4½in (A) (center round of Flying Geese)

From each of the five hand dyed fabrics you've chosen for the second round, cut:
• Eight rectangles, 2½in x 4½in (B) (second round of Flying Geese)

From an assortment of the hand dyed fabrics you have left, cut:
• 72 squares, 2½in (I) (Border 1)

From the commercial print fabric in autumn tones, cut:
• Two strips, 4½in x width of fabric. Cross cut them into four rectangles, 4½in x 20½in (F).
• Five strips, 4½in x width of fabric (Border 2)

From the dark commercial print fabric, cut:
• Three strips, 2½in x width of fabric. Cross cut them into 48 squares, 2½in (G) (center round of Flying Geese).
• Four strips, 2½in x width of fabric. Cross cut them into eight rectangles 2½in x 20½in (C).
• Five strips, 2½in x width of fabric. Cross cut them into 72 squares, 2½in (J) (Border 1).
• Six strips, 2¼in x width of fabric (binding)
• Two strips, 4½in x width of fabric. Cross cut them into four rectangles, 4½in x 8½in (D) and five squares, 4½in (E).

From the light commercial print fabric, cut:
• Five strips, 2½in x width of fabric. Cross cut them into 80 squares, 2½in (H) (second round of Flying Geese).

Easy ⬚ ⬚ ⬚

Designed by Gail Simpson; patchwork by Fay Winther; quilted by Rhonda Coates
Finished size: 52in (132cm) square

MAKE THE THREE DIMENSIONAL FLYING GEESE

The Flying Geese blocks are three dimensional, or 'Loose Goose', a technique first developed by Mary Ellen Hopkins. Refer to the diagrams for guidance.

1. Fold a hand dyed A rectangle in half, right side out and short edges matching.

2. Then sandwich it between two G squares, right sides facing in, aligning the raw edges at the bottom and sides. The folded edge of the rectangle is ¼in short of the raw edge of the squares at the top. This is the 'tip' of the goose. Repeat with all of the 24 A rectangles.

3. Sandwich each B rectangle between two H squares in the same manner. Repeat with all 40 B rectangles.

4. Stack all the prepared units ready for chain piecing. Stitch from the top down, over the inside fold.

5. Snip the fold inside the seam allowance, flattening it out completely. Finger press the goose section open, aligning the fold of the goose over the seam.

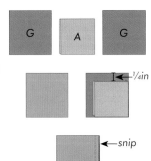

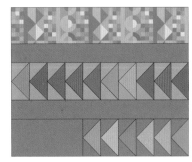

Making three dimensional Flying Geese

Tip

Do not press these Flying Geese at this stage, as it tends to distort their corners. Wait until you have sewn the Flying Geese into strips before pressing them.

MAKE THE LARGE BLOCKS

Large blocks – make 4

1. Although this quilt looks complex, it's actually constructed from four large blocks sewn around a center square. To make the large blocks, begin by laying out one of each of the six different colored A Flying Geese in a row, all facing the same direction. Join them together and press. See Diagram 1.

Diagram 1

Tip

When joining the units, be careful not to catch the tip of the 'goose' in the seam.

2. Join a D rectangle of dark commercial print fabric to one end of the strip – the end that the Flying Geese units appear to be pointing to. See Diagram 2. The strip should measure 20½in long, from raw edge to raw edge.

Diagram 2

3. Repeat with all of the remaining A Flying Geese and D background rectangles to make four units like this. They will be used in the center of the quilt. In *Autumn Geese*, all of the units are exactly the same, but you could mix and match the order of the Flying Geese in each unit if you wished.

4. Lay out two of each of the five different colored B Flying Geese in a row, all facing the same direction. See Diagram 3. Join them together and press. The strip should measure 20½in long, from raw edge to raw edge.

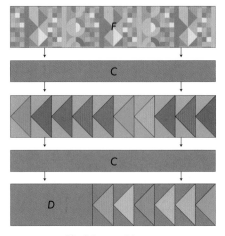

Diagram 3

5. Repeat with all of the remaining B Flying Geese to make four strips like this. Again, in *Autumn Geese* all the units are exactly the same, but you could mix and match the order of the Flying Geese if you wished.

Block Layout Diagram

6. Referring to the Block Layout Diagram, lay out an F autumn print strip, a C dark commercial print strip, a strip of B Flying Geese made in step 5, another C dark commercial print strip, and a strip of A Flying Geese + D strip, made in step 2. The Flying Geese should all be pointing in the same direction.

7. Sew the strips together along their long edges. Press seams away from the Flying Geese.

8. Repeat to make four blocks like this.

ASSEMBLE THE QUILT

1. Place an E dark commercial print fabric square on your design wall or work surface. Lay out the four large blocks around it, referring to the quilt photograph and the Quilt Center Layout Diagram for guidance.

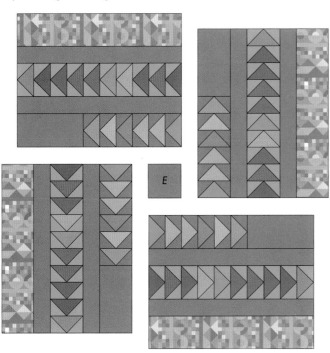

Quilt Center Layout Diagram

2. Start assembling the quilt by stitching Large Block 1 to the top edge of the centre E square. Use a partial seam only at this stage; that is, only stitch about 3in along the top of the E square, leaving the rest of the seam unstitched. See Diagram 4.

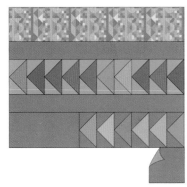

Diagram 4

3. Next, stitch Large Block 2 to the centre square and the short edge of Large Block 1. Press the seam towards Large Block 2.

4. In a similar manner join Large Block 3 and Large Block 4 to the center.

5. Finally, return to the first seam that you sewed between Large Block 1 and the center square. You can now complete the stitching, joining Large Block 1 to the top edge of the center square and the short end of Large Block 4. Your quilt should now measure 36½in square.

ADD BORDER 1

1. Lay out two I squares of hand dyed fabric and two J squares of dark commercial print fabric in two rows of two.

2. Sew pairs of squares together, then sew the pairs together to complete a Four-patch block.

3. Repeat with the remaining I and J squares to make 36 Four-patch blocks.

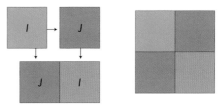

Four-patch block – make 36

4. Lay out nine Four-patch blocks in a row. Mix and match the blocks until you have an array of colors that you like. Then sew the blocks together to make a Border 1 strip. It should measure 36½in from end to end.

5. Repeat with the remaining Four-patch blocks to make four Border 1 strips.

6. Pin, then sew a Border 1 strip to the left and right edges of the quilt. Press seams towards the quilt center.

7. Sew an E square of dark commercial print fabric to each end of the remaining Border 1 strips, then sew them to the top and bottom edges of the quilt.

ADD BORDER 2

1. Join the five 4½in strips of commercial autumn print fabric end to end to make one long strip. If you join the strips on the diagonal, it helps to disguise the join.

2. Referring to Adding Borders in Quilting Basics, page 89, measure the quilt vertically, and trim two strips this length from the long strip. Sew them to the left and right edges of the quilt. Press seams towards the border strips.

3. Measure the quilt horizontally, and trim two strips this length from the long strip. Sew the strips to the top and bottom edges of the quilt.

FINISH THE QUILT

1. Cut the length of backing fabric in half. Remove the selvages. Referring to Piecing the Backing in Quilting Basics, page 89, join the two sections together, then trim to 60in square for the backing of the quilt.

2. Referring to Preparing the Quilt Sandwich in Quilting Basics, page 89, layer the backing, batting and quilt ready for quilting.

3. Quilt as desired. *Autumn Geese* was machine quilted by Rhonda Coates. She worked spirals, flowers and leaves in the center of the quilt and straight lines of stitching in the borders.

4. Join the six strips cut for the binding end to end to make one long strip. Use it to bind the quilt, referring to Binding the Quilt in Quilting Basics, page 89.

Birds and Bouquet Fantasy

I HAD BEEN LOOKING for a way to use the Bouquet block with hand dyed fabrics in bright colors. When I spied this fabulous print of fantasy birds and flowers, I realized that combined with a light background, I had what I needed – except a design! I saw the Migrating Geese technique in a book and was able to obtain permission to use it. This technique was given to Georgia Bonesteel by Pauline Adams. The Bouquet blocks feature three-dimensional patches and the appliqué is free-form, adding elements of whimsy to the quilt. You can use my original flower shapes or draw your own favorite flowers, birds or whatever works with the commercial print theme fabric you choose. Machine embroidery is another option.

MATERIALS

1¾yd (1.6m) multicolored commercial theme print fabric
3⅜yd (3.1m) light commercial print fabric
12 hand dyed fat eighths [9in x 21in (25cm x 55cm)] – six light and six dark. The colors used in *Birds and Bouquet Fantasy* as shown are: purple, pink, orange, yellow, green and blue.
5½yd (5m) roll of fusible ¼in (6mm)-wide bias tape (grey or green)
⅝yd (50cm) fusible web
Neutral thread for piecing
Rayon or cotton thread for appliqué in colors to match the flowers, leaves and vine
Template plastic and permanent marking pen
Rotary cutter, ruler and mat
Sewing machine and general sewing supplies

CUT THE FABRIC

From the multicolored commercial theme print fabric, cut:
• Six strips, 2½in x **length** of fabric (sashings)
• Four strips, 2¼in x **length** of fabric (binding)
• Three squares, 6⅝in. Cross cut each square once on the diagonal to yield six half-square triangles (A) (Migrating Geese).
• One square, 5in. Cross cut the square once on the diagonal to yield two half-square triangles (B) (Migrating Geese).
• Three squares, 6½in (G) (Bouquet blocks)
• Six squares, 2⅝in (H) squares
• Nine squares, 4in (I) (Bouquet blocks)
From the light commercial print fabric, cut:
• Two strips, 6½in x **length** of fabric (Border 1)

Advanced ☐ ☐ ☐

Designed and made by Gail Simpson; quilted by Rhonda Coates
Finished size: 53in x 73in (135cm x 186cm)

- Six strips, 6¼in x remaining width of fabric. Cross cut into 22 squares, 6¼in (C) (Migrating Geese).
- One square, 20in. Cross cut it on both diagonals to yield four quarter-square triangles (setting triangles).
- Two squares, 11in. Cross cut each square once on the diagonal to yield four half-square triangles (setting corners).
- Six squares, 6½in (K) (Bouquet blocks)
- Three squares, 4¼in. Cross cut each square on both diagonals to yield 12 quarter-square triangles (L) (Bouquet blocks).
- Three squares, 3⅞in. Cross cut each square once on the diagonal to yield six half-square triangles (M) (Bouquet blocks).
- Nine squares, 3½in (J) (Bouquet blocks)
- One square, 4in. Cross cut it once on the diagonal to yield two half-square triangles (F) (Migrating Geese).
- One rectangle 3¼in x 20in (Bouquet strip)
- One rectangle 8in x 20in (Bouquet strip)

From each of the six dark hand dyed fabrics, cut:
- Two squares, 3⅞in. Cross cut each square once on the diagonal to yield a total of 24 half-square triangles (O) (Bouquet blocks). You will use 18 in this project.
- One square, 6⅝in. Cross cut each square once on the diagonal to yield a total of 12 half-square triangles (D) (Migrating Geese). Only six triangles are used for the Migrating Geese. Put one triangle of each color aside to use for the appliqué.

From each of the six light hand dyed fabrics, cut:
- Two squares 3⅞in. Cross cut each square once on the diagonal to yield a total of 24 half-square triangles (N) (Bouquet blocks). You will use 18 in this project.
- One square, 6⅝in. Cross cut each square once on the diagonal to yield a total of 12 half-square triangles (E) (Migrating Geese).

Set aside the rest of the hand dyed fabrics (and six of the D triangles) for appliqué.

MAKE THE MIGRATING GEESE STRIPS

1. Fold each D and E triangle of hand dyed fabric in half and finger press the corner to crease lightly. Unfold the triangles and pin each one on a corner of a C square of light commercial print fabric, right sides together and edges aligned. See Diagram 1.

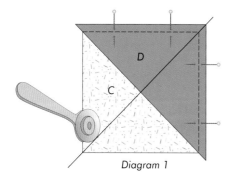

2. Stitch the two short edges of the triangles. Do not stitch into the seam allowance. When you come to the diagonal crease you made at the corner, leave the needle inserted in the fabric, lift the presser

foot and turn the fabric to stitch the second side. Cut the unit in half on the diagonal.

3. Open out the units to yield two Migrating Geese. They will be mirror images of each other. Finger press the seams towards the hand dyed fabrics and trim the corners.

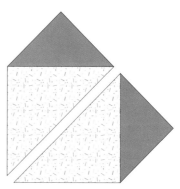

Migrating Geese units

4. Repeat steps 1-3 with the three A triangles of multicolored commercial theme print fabric and three C triangles. You will have one C triangle left. Cut it in half on the diagonal to yield two half-square triangles (½C).

5. The two strips of Migrating Geese are assembled from the bottom up. Referring to the diagrams, start with a B triangle of multicolored commercial theme print fabric, then add Migrating Geese units. In *Birds and Bouquet Fantasy* the Migrating Geese were in the color sequence yellow, orange, pink, purple, blue, green and the multicolor commercial theme print. There was a sequence of the light E hand dyed triangles, followed by a sequence of the dark D hand dyed triangles in the middle of the strip, and then another sequence of the light E hand dyed triangles at the top of the strip. Referring to the diagrams and

Diagram 1

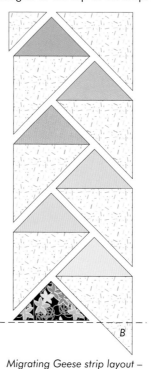
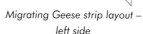

Migrating Geese strip layout – left side

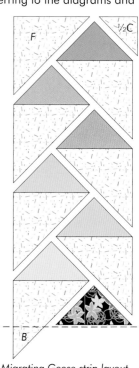

Migrating Geese strip layout – right side

the photograph of the finished quilt, lay out the units so that the strips are mirror images of each other.

5. Stitch the strips together by starting at the bottom of each strip. Sew the B triangle to the first Migrating Geese unit. Then stitch the next Migrating Geese unit to the edge of B+first Migrating Geese unit. Continue in this manner to sew all the units in each strip.

6. Complete the strips by sewing ½C and F triangles at the top corners. Then trim the top and bottom edges of the strips square.

7. Measure the length of the Migrating Geese strips. Trim four of the 2½in strips of multicolored commercial theme print fabric to this length. Sew one to the left and right edges of each Migrating Geese strip.

MAKE THE BOUQUET BLOCKS

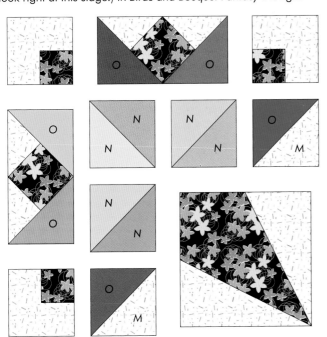

1. This block looks quite complex, but if you make smaller units first before stitching them together, it becomes much more straightforward. Lay out all the patches for a block, referring to the Block Layout Diagram. (The I squares for the corner units won't look right at this stage.) In *Birds and Bouquet Fantasy* the light

hand dyed fabrics were used in the middle of the block (N) and the dark hand dyed fabrics were used on the outer edges (O).

2. Begin by making the corner units. Fold an I square of multicolored commercial theme print fabric in half, then half again, wrong sides together, to make a multi-layered 2in square. See Diagram 2.

Diagram 2

3. Pin it in one corner of a J square, matching raw edges; the folded edges will be towards the center of the J square. Stay stitch in place ⅛in from the edges. Repeat to make three corner units like this.

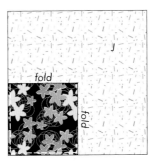

Corner units – make 3

4. The pieced squares in the center of the block are made by simply stitching the six N triangles together in pairs along their long edges. Make two more pieced squares by stitching O and M triangles together. Press the seams on these units open.

Block Layout Diagram

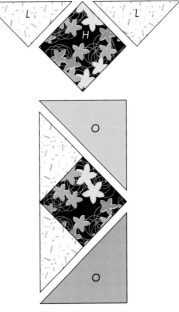

Side units – make 2

5. For the side units, begin by stitching the two light L triangles to the H square. Complete the unit by stitching an O triangle to the two shorter sides.

6. The 'cone' units are made using two Connectors. Refer to Connectors in Quilting Basics, page 89. On the wrong side of a K square, make a light pencil mark 3⅜in from the top right corner. Make a light pencil mark ⅛in from the bottom right corner. Draw a line connecting these marks as shown in Diagram 3.

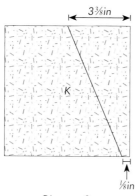

Diagram 3

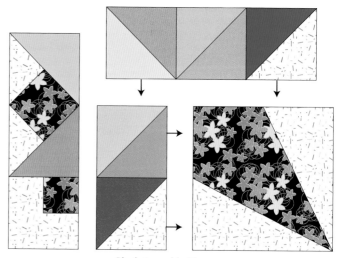

Block Assembly Diagram

7. Match the K square with a G square, right sides together and sew on the line. Fold the K square over to the right side and finger press. Trim the top layer of light fabric even with the edges of the G square. At this stage the corner of the block has three layers: two layers of the light fabric and one of the multicolored commercial print theme fabric. You need to decide whether to trim the middle layer. If the theme fabric would show through the top layer of light fabric, don't trim the middle layer.

8. Repeat steps 6 and 7, but this type mark the K square in mirror reverse, as shown in Diagram 4.

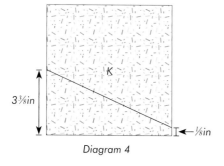

Diagram 4

9. To assemble the block, stitch the pieced squares together in one row of three and one column of two. Stitch the column to the left edge of the cone unit. Stitch the row of three to the top edge.

10. Stitch a corner unit to a side unit. Stitch this to the left edge of the block. Stitch the remaining two corner units to the left and right edges of the remaining side unit and stitch to the top of the block.

11. Repeat steps 1 – 10 to make three Bouquet blocks. Note that Gail varies the color placement in each of her blocks.

ASSEMBLE THE QUILT

1. Lay out the three Bouquet blocks and the setting triangles, referring to Diagonal Setting in Quilting Basics, page 89.

2. Sew the setting triangles and blocks together in diagonal rows. Handle the setting triangles with care as you will be sewing bias edges. Finger press the seams.

3. Then sew the rows together, carefully matching seams. Add the half-square corner triangles at each end of the strip. All the setting triangles have been cut over size to allow the Bouquet blocks to 'float' on the background. Trim the assembled strip to square up the corners and reduce the float to a size that you like.

4. Measure the width of the Bouquet strip. Trim the 3¼in x 20in rectangle and the 8in x 20in rectangle of light commercial print fabric to this width. Sew the 3¼in rectangle to the top edge of the strip and the 8in rectangle to the bottom edge. See Diagram 5.

5. Measure the length of the Migrating Geese strips. Measure the length of the Bouquet strip. Trim the bottom edge of the Bouquet strip to make it the same length as the Migrating Geese strips.

6. Sew a Migrating Geese strip to the left and right edges of the Bouquet strip. Refer to the photograph of *Birds and Bouquet Fantasy* before stitching to ensure that you are sewing the Migrating Geese strips to the correct edge.

7. Measure the width of the quilt. Trim the remaining two 2½in strips of multicolored commercial print theme fabric to this length and sew them to the top and bottom edges.

ADD THE BORDER

1. Referring to Adding Borders in Quilting Basics, page 89, measure the quilt vertically and trim a strip this length from both of the 6½in strips of light commercial print fabric.

2. Appliqué these border strips before joining them to the quilt. This will make the appliqué easier to maneuver if you stitch by

machine, and will also allow you to place the raw edges of the stems in the seam allowance, and have them caught in the seams. Instructions are provided for machine appliqué using fusible web but the design lends itself to a variety of appliqué techniques. Adapt the instructions for the appliqué method of your choice.

3. Referring to the quilt photograph as a guide, cut various lengths of iron-on bias tape for the vines. Position one end of each vine so that it matches the raw edges of the border strip. Fuse the tape to the fabric and stitch in place. In *Birds and Bouquet Fantasy* the vines were appliquéd by machine using a serpentine stitched worked in green rayon thread.

4. Trace the shapes for the flowers, flower centers and leaves from page 61 – or draw your own – onto the paper side of the fusible web. Leave at least 1/2in between shapes. Cut the shapes out about 1/4in outside the traced lines.

5. Iron the fusible web shapes onto the wrong side of the remaining pieces of hand dyed fabrics. Using the quilt photograph as a guide, arrange the shapes for the flowers and leaves on the border strips. Remove the paper backing from the shapes and fuse them in place. Appliqué them using your preferred appliqué method and thread of choice.

6. Sew the appliquéd borders to the left and right edges of the quilt.

7. Measure the quilt horizontally and trim the remains of the two 6 1/2in strips of light commercial print fabric to this length. Repeat steps 3 – 5 to appliqué them, then stitch them to the top and bottom edges of the quilt.

8. Complete any appliqué that overlaps border seams.

FINISH THE QUILT

1. Cut the length of backing fabric in half. Remove the selvages. Referring to Piecing the Backing in Quilting Basics, page 89, join the sections, then trim to 57in x 77in for the backing of the quilt.

2. Referring to Preparing the Quilt Sandwich in Quilting Basics, page 89, layer the backing, batting and quilt ready for quilting. Thread or pin-baste.

3. Quilt as desired. *Birds and Bouquet Fantasy* was machine quilted by Kim Bradley. She 'McTavished' in the background of the Bouquet blocks, stippled small bouquet blocks in the setting triangles and worked flowers in the rectangles at the top and bottom of the Bouquet strip. The Migrating Geese strips were quilted in the light commercial print patches only with a scallop pattern. The borders were quilted with flowers and leaves.

4. Join the four strips cut for the binding to make one long strip. Use it to bind the quilt, referring to Binding the Quilt in Quilting Basics, page 89.

Diagram 5

Fun with Nine-patch

EVEN THE SIMPLEST OF PATTERNS can come alive using wonderful hand dyed fabrics and just the right printed fabric. Have fun making easy Nine-patch blocks, then cut them up and reassemble them to create a much more complex block with no effort at all. This quilt was designed using two hand dyed fabrics and one commercial print fabric for the blocks. Choose a light hand dyed fabric or commercial print for the background. Alternate blocks can be embroidered, appliquéd or left plain.

MATERIALS

1⅝yd (1.4m) commercial print fabric (blocks and border). If using a directional print, 1¾yd (1.6m) will be needed.

¼yd (25cm) scarlet hand dyed fabric (blocks)

⅜yd (30cm) ochre hand dyed fabric (blocks)

1¼yd (1m) light hand dyed or commercial print fabric (alternate blocks and setting triangles)

2⅞yd (2.6m) backing fabric

50in x 62in (127cm x 157cm) batting

Rayon machine embroidery threads to complement the commercial print fabric (if embellishing the alternate squares with machine embroidery)

Neutral thread for piecing

Rotary cutter, ruler and mat

Sewing machine and general sewing supplies

Note: Pfaff Embroidery Card 359, designs 11 and 12 were used for the embroidery.

CUT THE FABRIC

From the commercial print fabric, cut:

Non-directional print
• Four strips, 5in x **length** of fabric (borders)
• Three strips, 4in x **length** of fabric. Cross cut into 48 rectangles, 3in x 4in (blocks).
• Four strips, 2¼in x **length** of fabric (binding)

Directional print
• Three strips, 5in x width of fabric (top and bottom borders)
• Two strips, 5in x remaining **length** of fabric (left and right borders)
• Four strips, 4in x remaining **length** of fabric. Cross cut into 48 rectangles, 3in x 4in (blocks).
• Five strips, 2¼in x remaining **length** of fabric (binding)

From the scarlet hand dyed fabric, cut:
• One strip, 3in x width of fabric. Cross cut into 14 squares, 3in (blocks).
• One strip, 4in x width of fabric. Cross cut into eight squares, 4in (blocks). Trim the rest of the strip to 3in wide, and from it cut another two squares, 3in to make a total of 16 squares, 3in (blocks).

Designed and made by Gail Simpson; quilted by Kim Bradley
Finished size: 44½in x 55¾in (113cm x 142cm)
Finished block size: 8in

From the ochre hand dyed fabric, cut:
- Two strips, 3in x width of fabric. Cross cut into 28 squares, 3in (blocks).
- One strip, 4in x width of fabric. Cross cut into four squares, 4in (blocks). Trim the rest of the strip to 3in wide, and from it cut another four squares, 3in to make a total of 32 squares, 3in (blocks).

From the light hand dyed or commercial print fabric, cut:
- Two strips, 9in x width of fabric. Cross cut into six squares, 9in (alternate blocks). These squares are cut oversize and then trimmed to size after completing the surface work. This eliminates any potential problems arising from 'shrinkage'.
- Two squares, 7½in. Cut each square once on the diagonal to yield four half-square triangles (corners).
- One strip, 13½in x width of fabric. Cross cut into three squares, 13½in. Cut each square on both diagonals to yield 12 quarter-square triangles (setting triangles). Only 10 will be used in this project.

MAKE THE BLOCKS

Block 1 – make 8

Block 2 – make 4

1. Lay out four 3in ochre squares, one 4in scarlet square and four rectangles of the commercial print fabric as shown for Block 1. Join the patches in each row together, then join the rows, carefully matching seams. Repeat to make eight Block 1.

2. In a similar manner, lay out four 3in scarlet squares, one 4in ochre square and four rectangles of the commercial print fabric as shown for Block 2. Join the patches in each row together, then join the rows, carefully matching seams. Repeat to make four Block 2.

3. Now for the fun part! Working with one block at a time, cross cut horizontally and vertically through the center of each block to form four units. See Diagram 1.

Diagram 1

4. Rearrange the four units as shown in Diagram 2. Join the units together in pairs, then join the pairs together to form a new block. Repeat with all Block 1 and Block 2.

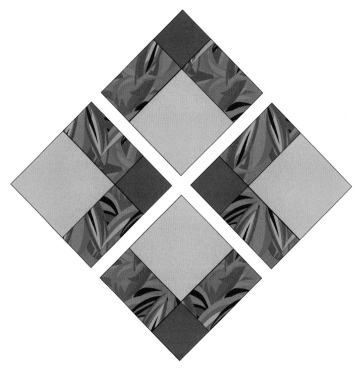

Diagram 2

MAKE THE EMBROIDERED OR APPLIQUÉD BLOCKS

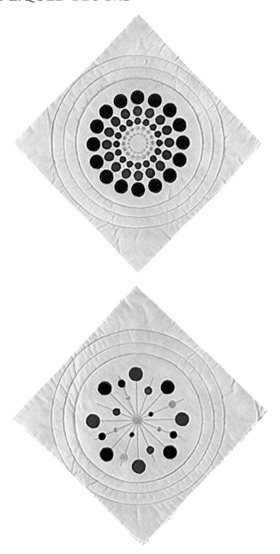

1. Embroider or appliqué the six 9in squares of light background fabric. Machine embroideries from Pfaff Card 359, designs 011 and 012 were used in *Fun with Nine-patch*. These designs were chosen to complement the rigid lines of the pieced blocks. The thread colors selected echo the colors of the commercial print fabric. Refer to the manual for your sewing machine for embroidery instructions.

2. Alternatively, you may prefer to appliqué these blocks. Some suggested motifs are included on the next page. Choose elements that will suit the theme suggested by the commercial print fabric you have chosen. Refer to Quilting Basics, page 89, for help with the appliqué.

3. Trim the finished blocks to 8½in square.

ASSEMBLE THE QUILT

The setting triangles have been cut slightly oversized. This creates a narrow border of background fabric around the edge of the quilt center: it allows the blocks to 'float' with a little 'breathing space'. Take care not to stretch the bias edges of these triangles as you work.

1. Referring to Diagonal Setting in Quilting Basics, page 89, lay out the pieced and alternate blocks in diagonal rows. Note that all of the Block 2 are in the center column of blocks. Add the setting triangles. Join the triangles and blocks in each diagonal row together.

2. Join the rows together, matching the block seams.

3. Add the corner triangles last. Press and trim overlap as required.

ADD THE BORDERS

1. Referring to Adding Borders in Quilting Basics, page 89, measure the quilt vertically. Trim two long strips of commercial print fabric to this length. Pin, then sew them to the left and right edges of the quilt. Press the seams towards the border strips.

2. In the same manner, measure the quilt horizontally. Trim the two remaining strips of commercial print fabric to this length. (If you are using a directional print, join the three 5in strips cut across the width of the fabric end to end to make one long strip. Cut the two strips you need for the top and bottom borders from it.) Pin, then sew them to the top and bottom edges of the quilt. Press the seams towards the border strips.

FINISH THE QUILT

1. Cut the length of backing fabric in half. Remove the selvages. Join the two sections, referring to Piecing the Backing in Quilting Basics, page 89, then trim to 50in x 62in for the backing of the quilt.

2. Referring to Preparing the Quilt Sandwich in Quilting Basics, page 89, layer the backing, batting and quilt ready for quilting. Thread or pin-baste.

3. Quilt as desired. *Fun with Nine-patch* was machine quilted by Kim Bradley. The pieced blocks were quilted with a freehand feather design radiating from the center out to each corner. The embroidered blocks were echo quilted with circles, and the setting triangles worked with a freehand flame design. The borders were quilted with feathers.

4. Join the four strips cut for the binding end to end to make one long strip. Use it to bind the quilt, referring to Binding the Quilt in Quilting Basics, page 89.

These motifs are provided as possible appliqué shapes for the alternate blocks in your quilt. Choose strong colors with the stars and moons for a bold boy's quilt. The hearts and flowers in pastel hand dyed fabrics would be delightful on a pretty girl's quilt. The lizard could be used to complement an ethnic print. Use your imagination to create embellishments for the alternate squares in your quilt that work well with the commercial print fabric you have chosen.

Not Quite 1000 Pyramids

Designed and made by Gail Simpson
Finished size: 50in x 65½in (127cm x 166cm)

Not Quite 1000 Pyramids

THIS QUILT IS SO MUCH FUN TO MAKE. *The pieced border has been made from leftover block trimmings. The final border has raw edge triangles stitched here and there. To top it off, quilting is a breeze, with the ricrac providing a nice finishing touch.*

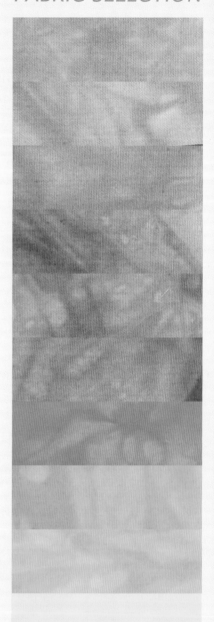

MATERIALS

10 bright hand dyed fat eighths [9in x 21in (25cm x 55cm)]
2¼yd (2m) multicolor striped commercial print fabric
1⅛yd (1m) plain black fabric
4½yd (4m) black ricrac trim
3¼yd (2.8m) backing fabric
Batting at least 54in x 71in (137cm x 176cm)
Nifty Notions 45 degree Kaleidoscope Ruler or templates made using the shapes on page 37
Template plastic and black permanent marking pen
Neutral sewing thread for piecing; monofilament thread for quilting
Sewing thread to match ricrac trim
Rotary cutter, ruler and mat
Sewing machine
General sewing supplies

CUT THE FABRIC

1. Begin by tracing Template B from page 37 onto template plastic using a black permanent marking pen. Cut out the template just inside the line.
2. If you are not using a Kaleidoscope Ruler, repeat this process to make Template A. From each of the 10 hand dyed fabrics, cut:
• One strip, 8in x width of fabric (21in). From it, cross cut one Template B, three triangles using the Kaleidoscope Ruler or Template A and then another Template B. See Diagram 1.

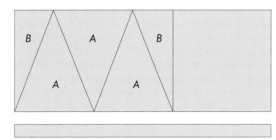

Diagram 1

Note: When using hand dyed fabrics, reversing the templates is not necessary to create mirror images of shapes, as the fabric is the same on both sides. Once the shape has been cut out, it can be turned over when the instructions require Template B-reversed. If you ever decide to make this quilt using only commercial print fabrics, cut half of the B triangles with the templates reversed.

Intermediate

Set all the remaining hand dyed fabrics aside for Border 4. From the multicolor striped commercial print fabric, cut:

- Two strips, 6in x width of fabric (Border 4)
- Two strips, 6in x **remaining length** of fabric (Border 4)
- Five strips, 8in x 30in (remaining width). Fold three of these strips in half, short edges matching and right sides together. At the raw edge end of the three doubled strips, cut one Template B, to yield three B and three B-reversed. Unfold the strips and from the length that remains and from the other two strips, cross cut triangles using the Kaleidoscope Ruler or Template A to yield 27 triangles.
- One strip, 8in x 30in. Trim the end of the strip at a 45 degree angle using the Kaleidoscope Ruler or Template A. Then cross cut into 13 strips, 2in. See Diagram 2.

Diagram 2

From the black fabric, cut:

- Four strips, 1½in x width of fabric (Border 1)
- Three strips, 1½in x width of fabric. Cross cut into 12 rectangles, 1½in x 8in (Border 2).
- Five strips, 1in x width of fabric (Border 3)
- One strip, 6in x width of fabric. Cross cut four squares, 6in (Border 4 corners). Trim the rest of the strip to 4in wide and cross cut four squares, 4in (Border 2 corners).
- Six strips, 2¼in x width of fabric (binding)

MAKE THE ROWS

Each rows has nine triangles (A) and two half triangles (B).

1. Using the photograph of the quilt and Diagram 3 as a guide, arrange the triangles in six rows. Rows 1, 3 and 5 begin and end with striped fabric half triangles; rows 2, 4 and 6 begin and end with hand dyed fabric half triangles. When you are happy with your color arrangement, join the triangles in each row together. Note that you will have some hand dyed B triangles left over; they will be used in Border 2.

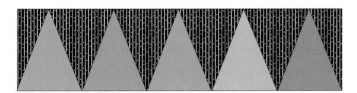

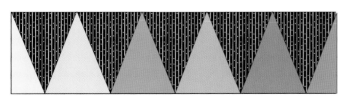

Diagram 3

2. Finger press the rows. Do not use the iron at this stage as you may stretch the fabrics. Press the seam allowances in rows 1, 3 and 5 to the left and in rows 2, 4 and 6 to the right.

3. Join the rows to form the quilt center. Gently press all seams towards the bottom edge of the quilt. Some trimming may be necessary to straighten up the sides. If so, trim ¼in outside the point of the half triangle. See Diagram 4.

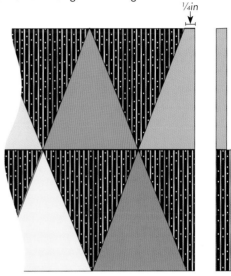

Diagram 4

ADD BORDER 1

1. Referring to Adding Borders in Quilting Basics, page 89, join the 1½in black strips end to end to make one long strip.

2. Measure the length of the quilt and cut two strips this length from the black strip. Sew them to the left and right edges of the quilt.

3. Measure the width of the quilt and cut two strips this length from the black strip. Sew them to the top and bottom edges of the quilt. Press the seams towards the border.

ADD BORDER 2

1. Chose 28 of the remaining B triangles cut from hand dyed fabrics to use in this border. Stitch one of the 2in strips of multicolor striped fabric between two hand dyed B triangles to make Unit 1 (see diagram). Repeat to make 14 Unit 1.

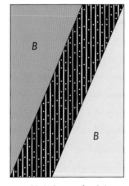

Unit 1 – make 14

2. Lay out the Unit 1 in one row of six Units and one row of eight Units. Insert a 1½ x 8in black rectangle between the Units in each row, and stitch the Units and rectangles in each row together.

Press all the seams in one direction. The top and bottom edges of the strips will not be straight. Trim them so that they are the same width and as wide as possible (approximately 7¾in).

3. Cut each of the pieced strips in half down their length, to yield two long strips and two short strips, all about 3⅜in wide. See Diagram 5.

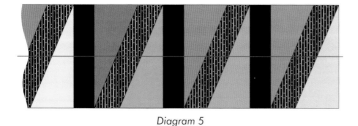

Diagram 5

4. Measure the quilt vertically. Trim the two long strips to this length. Measure the quilt horizontally. Trim the two short strips to this length.

5. Sew the longer pieced strips to the left and right edges of the quilt. Press seams towards Border 1.

6. Trim the four black 4in squares so that they are the same height and width as the pieced strips. Sew a black square to each end of the pieced border strips. Sew the strips to the top and bottom edges of the quilt.

ADD BORDER 3

1. This border is a 'peeper strip' – a folded flap – sewn into the seam between Borders 2 and 4. The folded edge of the strip is not sewn down.

2. Join the 1in strips of black fabric end to end to make one long strip. Press the seams open. Fold the strip in half, long edges matching and wrong sides together, and press.

3. Measure the quilt vertically and cut two strips this length from the black strip. Measure the quilt horizontally and cut two strips this length from the black strip.

4. Match the raw edges of the two longer black folded strips with the raw edges on the left and right edges of the quilt and stitch.

5. Match the raw edges of the two shorter black folded strips with the raw edges on the top and bottom edges of the quilt and stitch.

ADD BORDER 4

1. For the corners, cut four triangles from the striped background fabric small enough to fit inside a 5½in square. Cut them freehand, using just a ruler and rotary cutter – no templates. Each triangle will be slightly different from the others.

2. In a similar manner, cut four triangles from hand dyed fabrics small enough to fit inside the striped background triangles cut in step 1. You can cut these from the leftover B triangles or the remaining strips of hand dyed fabrics.

3. Place a striped triangle diagonally across a black 6in square. Stitch around the triangle using a narrow blanket stitch. Place a hand dyed triangle on top of the striped triangle and top stitch in place ¼in inside the raw edges using a contrasting thread. Repeat to make four corner blocks.

4. Cut another 36 freehand triangles from the remaining hand dyed fabric strips and B triangles. They should be about 2½in

– 3in high. Place them in a scattered fashion on the striped Border 4 strips, at least ½in from the edge of the strips. Top stitch them in place ¼in from the raw edges using a contrasting thread.

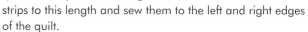

5. Referring to Adding Borders in Quilting Basics, page 89, measure the quilt vertically. Trim the longer border strips to this length and sew them to the left and right edges of the quilt.

6. Measure the quilt horizontally. Trim the shorter strips to this length. Join a black appliquéd square to each end of these Border 4 strips, being careful to orientate them correctly. Sew these strips to the top and bottom edges of the quilt.

FINISH THE QUILT

1. Cut the length of backing fabric in half. Remove the selvages. Referring to Piecing the Backing in Quilting Basics, page 89, join the two sections, then trim to 55in x 70in for the backing of the quilt.

2. Referring to Preparing the Quilt Sandwich in Quilting Basics, page 89, layer the backing, batting and quilt ready for quilting.

3. Quilt as desired. The center of Not Quite 1000 Pyramids was machine quilted in the ditch of the diagonal seams in both directions, starting and finishing under the Border 3 peeper strips.

4. Pin the ricrac onto the surface in a random pattern starting and ending again under the Border 3 peeper strips. Stitch in place using a straight or narrow zigzag stitch and thread to match the ricrac. Work freehand if desired.

5. The outer border was quilted in a freehand meander, avoiding the appliquéd triangles.

6. Join the six strips cut for the binding end to end to make one long strip. Use it to bind the quilt, referring to Binding the Quilt in Quilting Basics, page 89.

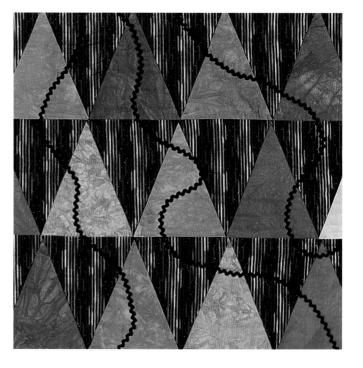

If you're looking for ways to use up scraps of fabrics left over from your projects, a miniature version of Not Quite 1000 Pyramids would be a fun idea. Make templates by cutting the base on the marked broken line, and assemble your mini as per the instructions provided for the larger quilt.

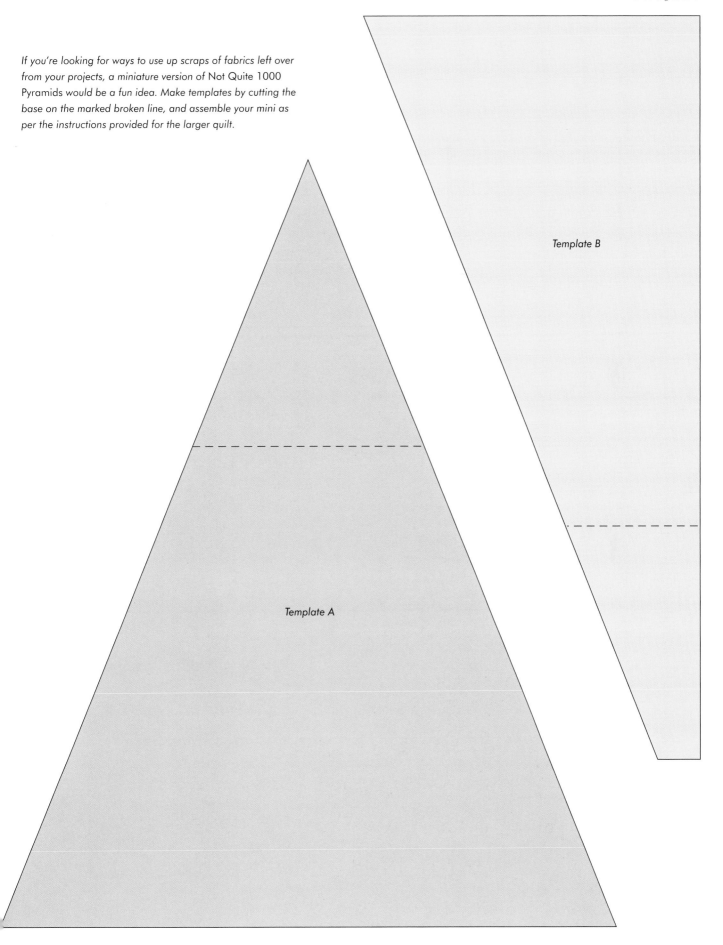

Template B

Template A

Federation Medallion

FEDERATION MEDALLION *is a good beginner quilt using only squares and triangles. It is based on a 3in grid, ensuring the pieces are not too small for a novice who is using these techniques for the first time. The quilt is embellished with machine embroidery in some of the patches. You could embroider by hand if you prefer, or even add an appliquéd design of your choice instead.*

MATERIALS

10 hand dyed fat eighths [9in x 21in (25cm x 55cm)]. They should be a light and dark in each of five different colors. The colors used in *Federation Medallion* as shown are: light purple, dark purple, light blue, dark blue, light red, dark red, light green, dark green, light gold and dark gold.

1yd (90cm) light commercial print fabric

1yd (90cm) medium-light commercial print fabric

3yd (2.6m) backing fabric

Batting at least 50in (130cm) square

Neutral thread for piecing

Rotary cutter, ruler and mat

Sewing machine and general supplies

Note: The embroidery design used on the blank blocks is Pfaff Card 28, design 009.

CUT THE FABRIC

From the dark green hand dyed fabric, cut:
- One square, 7¼in (Unit 2)
- Six squares, 3½in (Kansas Dugout blocks – Border 3)

From the light green hand dyed fabric, cut:
- Four squares, 3⅞in (Unit 2)
- Four squares, 3½in (Kansas Dugout blocks – Border 3)

From the dark blue hand dyed fabric, cut:
- Two squares, 3⅞in (Unit 3)
- Six squares, 3½in (Unit 3 and Kansas Dugout blocks – Border 3)

From the light blue hand dyed fabric, cut:
- Eight squares, 3½in (Unit 3 and Kansas Dugout blocks – Border 3)
- Two squares, 6in (Border 4 corners)

From the dark purple hand dyed fabric, cut:
- Two squares, 3⅞in (Unit 3)
- Six squares, 3½in (Unit 3 and Kansas Dugout blocks – Border 3)

From the light purple hand dyed fabric, cut:
- Eight squares, 3½in (Unit 3 and Kansas Dugout blocks – Border 3)
- Two squares, 6in (Border 4 corners)

From the dark red hand dyed fabric, cut:
- Four squares, 3⅞in (Unit 2)
- Four squares, 3½in (Kansas Dugout blocks – Border 3)

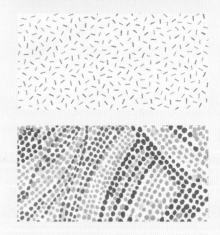

Easy

Designed and made by Gail Simpson; quilted by Kim Bradley
Finished size: 46in x 46in (117cm x 117cm)

From the light red hand dyed fabric, cut:
• Four squares, 3½in (Kansas Dugout blocks – Border 3)
From the dark gold hand dyed fabric, cut:
• Eight squares, 3½in (Unit 1 and Kansas Dugout blocks – Border 3)
From the light gold hand dyed fabric, cut:
• Six squares, 3½in (Unit 1 and Kansas Dugout blocks – Border 3)
From the light commercial print fabric, cut:
• Two strips, 3½in x width of fabric. Cross cut into 16 squares, 3½in (Unit 3).
• One strip, 3⅞in x width of fabric. Cross cut into eight squares, 3⅞in (Unit 2 and Unit 3).
• One strip, 5¼in x width of fabric. Cross cut into four squares, 5¼in (embroidered squares in Unit 2).
• Two strips, 2in x width of fabric. Cross cut into 44 squares, 2in (Kansas Dugout blocks – Border 3). If your strips are a little too short to allow you to cut 44 squares, use some of the leftover pieces from the 5¼in strip to cut the rest.
• Two strips, 2½in x 26½in and 2 strips, 2½in x 30½in (Border 2)
• Five strips, 2¼in x width of fabric (binding)
From the medium-light commercial print fabric, cut:
• Four strips, 5½in x width of fabric (Border 4)
• Two strips, 1½in x 24½in and two strips, 1½in x 26½in (Border 1)
• Two strips, 2in x width of fabric. Cross cut into 40 squares, 2in (Kansas Dugout blocks – Border 3).

MAKE THE CENTER

Although this center section looks complex, it can be made easily by assembling patches into three different kinds of units and then joining the units together.

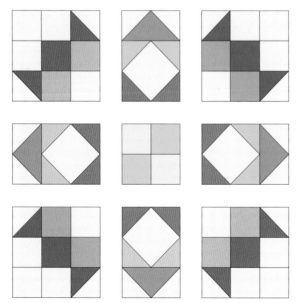

Block Assembly Diagram

1. Join a light gold 3½in square and a dark gold 3½in square. Repeat to make a second pair of squares, then join them as shown in the diagram to make a Four-patch block (Unit 1).
2. Complete the embroidery or other embellishment on the four 5¼in squares of light commercial print fabric. Position all

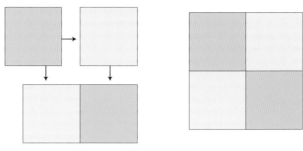

Four-patch block (Unit 1) – make 1

elements of your design at least ½in from the raw edges of the squares to allow for trimming and seams, and consider the position of the squares in your finished quilt when deciding on the orientation of your embellishments. Of course, you can leave these squares blank if you prefer. Press the squares, then trim them back to 4¾in square.
3. Cut the four light green and the four dark red 3⅞in squares in half along one diagonal. Sew a light green and a dark red triangle to opposite sides of each embellished square. Sew another light green and another dark red triangle to the remaining sides of each square. See Diagram 1.

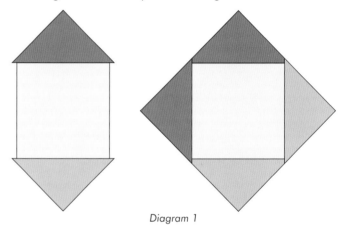

Diagram 1

4. Cut the dark green 7¼in square on both diagonals to give four quarter-square triangles. Cut four of the 3⅞in light commercial print fabric squares on one diagonal to give eight half-square triangles. Join a light commercial print fabric triangle to the short sides of the dark green triangles to make four Flying Geese. Join the Flying Geese to the squares from step 3 to make Unit 2: the Flying Geese should be sewn to the side of the square that has two light green triangles.
5. Draw a diagonal line on the wrong side of the four remaining light commercial print 3⅞in squares. Pair these squares with two dark blue and two dark purple 3⅞in squares, right sides together. Sew a seam ¼in on either side of the drawn line, and then cut on the line to yield a total of eight pieced squares.

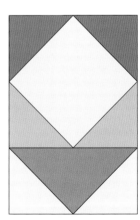

Unit 2 – make 4

6. To make a blue Unit 3, you will need:
• four 3½in squares of light commercial print fabric
• one 3½in square of dark blue fabric
• two pieced squares from step 5, both with made with dark blue fabric
• two 3½in square patches of light blue fabric

7. Referring to the diagram, lay out these patches in three rows of three patches each. Sew the patches together in rows. Then sew the rows together, carefully matching seams. Repeat to make another blue Unit 3.

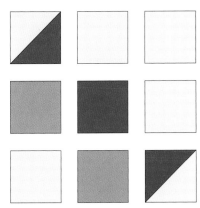

Unit 3 – make 2 blue and 2 purple

8. Repeat steps 6 and 7 to make two Unit 3 with dark and light purple patches.

9. Following the Block Assembly diagram, lay out the Four-patch block (Unit 1), the Unit 2 and the Unit 3 in three rows of three units each. The blue Unit 3 should be in diagonally opposite corners. Join the Units in each row together, then join the rows, carefully matching seams. Press gently. Your quilt should now measure 24½in from raw edge to raw edge.

ADD BORDERS 1 AND 2

1. Referring to Adding Borders in Quilting Basics, page 89, pin, then sew the two 1½in x 24½in strips of medium-light commercial print fabric to the left and right edges of the quilt center. Press seam allowances towards the border strips.

2. In the same manner, pin, then sew the 1½in x 26½in strips of medium-light commercial print fabric to the top and bottom edges of the quilt center. Press seam allowances towards the border strips.

3. Repeat this process with the 2½in strips cut from the light commercial print fabric for Border 2.

ADD BORDER 3

1. Border 3 is comprised of Kansas Dugout blocks, made using the Connector Method. Refer to Quilting Basics, page 89, for a description of this method.

2. Join one 2in square of light commercial print fabric and one 2in square of medium-light commercial print fabric to opposite corners of the remaining 3½in squares of hand dyed fabrics to complete a Kansas Dugout block. You will need to make 44 blocks all together: six dark green, six dark gold, and four each of light green, light gold, dark blue, light blue, dark purple, light purple, dark red and light red.

Kansas Dugout block – make 44

3. Referring to the diagram for color placement, lay out two sets of 10 Kansas Dugout blocks for the top and bottom strips of Border 3. Sew the blocks in each strip together. Pin, then sew these strips to the top and bottom edges of the quilt.

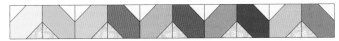

Border 3 – strips for the top and bottom edges – make 2

4. Join the remaining 24 blocks into two strips of 12 blocks each, referring to the diagram for color placement. Pin, then sew these strips to the left and right edges of the quilt. Press seam allowances towards the border strips.

Border 3 – strips for the left and right edges – make 2

ADD BORDER 4

1. Measure the width and the length of the quilt and trim the four 5½in strips of medium-light commercial print fabric to this length.

2. Pin, then sew strips to the left and right edges of the quilt.

3. If desired, embroider the two 6in squares of light purple fabric and the two 6in squares of light blue fabric and trim to 5½in square. Alternatively, appliqué a design of your choice or leave the squares plain. Remember to trim them to 5½in square whatever you decide to do.

4. Sew a purple and a blue 5½in square to each end of the remaining Border 4 strips.

5. Pin, then sew these strips to the top and bottom edges of the quilt.

FINISH THE QUILT

1. Cut the length of backing fabric in half. Remove the selvages. Referring to Piecing the Backing in Quilting Basics, page 89, join the two sections, then trim to 50in square for the backing of the quilt.

2. Referring to Preparing the Quilt Sandwich in Quilting Basics, page 89, layer the backing, batting and quilt ready for quilting.

3. Quilt as desired. *Federation Medallion* was free machine quilted by Kim Bradley. She worked a gentle curved design in the center block, a variety of looped designs on the light commercial print, and a continuous staggered half-heart design on Border 4.

4. Join the five strips cut for the binding end to end to make one long strip. Use it to bind the quilt, referring to Binding the Quilt in Quilting Basics, page 89.

For the Print

THE FULL TITLE OF THIS QUILT *is actually* For the Print I Could Not Cut Into Little Pieces. *When it is hard to cut up a much-loved commercial print fabric, but you have decided that it just has to be used, this quilt is the ideal answer. Take some time to gather the perfect hand dyed fabrics and use the precious fabric in large pieces to preserve the printed pattern as much as possible.*

MATERIALS

1yd (90cm) of a precious commercial print fabric (Border 2)

1yd (90cm) black and white striped commercial print fabric (sashings and Border 1). In *For the Print* this fabric has been cut so that the stripes in the sashings run vertically. If you decide not to use a striped print, only ¼yd (20cm) is needed.

½yd (50cm) dark grey hand dyed fabric (blocks and sashings)

⅜yd (35cm) light grey hand dyed fabric (blocks)

⅝yd (60cm) red hand dyed fabric (blocks)

¼yd (20cm) dark aqua hand dyed fabric (Border 1)

⅜yd (30cm) medium aqua hand dyed fabric (blocks and sashings)

¼yd (20cm) light aqua hand dyed fabric (blocks)

Batting at least 43in x 52in (109cm x 132cm)

1⅝yd (1.4m) backing fabric

Neutral thread for piecing; monofilament thread (quilting)

Rayon machine embroidery thread to contrast with the blocks (quilting)

Rotary cutter, ruler amd mat

Sewing machine

General sewing supplies

CUT THE FABRIC

From the precious commercial print fabric, cut:
- Two strips, 6½in x width of fabric (Border 2)
- Two strips, 2in x width of fabric (Border 2)
- Five strips, 2¼in x width of fabric (binding)

From the black and white striped commercial print, cut:
- Two strips, 1½in x **length** of fabric (sashing)
- One strip, 1½in x remaining width of fabric (Border 1)

If you are not using a striped fabric, just cut three strips, 1½in x width of fabric for the sashing and Border 1.

From the dark grey hand dyed fabric, cut:
- One strip, 8½in x width of fabric. Cross cut into 12 rectangles, 2½in x 8½in (blocks).
- One strip, 2½in x width of fabric. Cut the strip in half to create two half-strips, 2½in x about 21in (blocks).
- One strip, 4in x width of fabric (sashing)

From the light grey hand dyed fabric cut:
- One strip, 8½in x width of fabric. Cross cut into 16 rectangles, 2½in x 8½in (blocks).
- One strip, 2½in x width of fabric. Cut the strip in half to create two half-strips, 2½in x about 21in (blocks).

From the red hand dyed fabric, cut:
- One strip, 8½in x width of fabric. Cross cut into eight rectangles, 2½in x 8½in and two rectangles, 2½in x 11in (blocks).

Advanced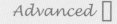

Designed and made by Gail Simpson
Finished size: approximately 39in x 48in (99cm x 122cm). Because this project involves
free cutting, the dimensions of your quilt may be slightly different from these.

- One strip, 4½in x width of fabric. Cut the strip in half to create two half-strips, 4½in x about 21in (blocks).
- Two strips, 4in x width of fabric (sashing)

From the dark aqua hand dyed fabric, cut:

- Two strips, 2½in x width of fabric (Border 1)

From the medium aqua hand dyed fabric, cut:

- One strip, 4½in x width of fabric. Cross cut into one rectangle, 4½in x 11in and one rectangle, 4½ x 8½in (blocks).
- One strip, 4in x width of fabric (sashing)

From the light aqua hand dyed fabric cut:

- Two strips, 2½in x width of fabric. Cross cut into six rectangles, 2½in x 8½in (blocks).

MAKE THE BLOCKS

1. Make four strip sets and cut them into segments. Refer to the diagrams below.

For Strip Set 1, sew a 2½in dark grey half-strip to either side of a 4½in red half-strip. Cross cut this strip set into six segments, 2½in wide.

For Strip Set 2, sew a 2½in light grey half-strip to either side of a 4½in red half-strip. Cross cut this strip set into eight segments, 2½in wide.

For Strip Set 3, sew a 2½in x 11in red strip to either side of the 4½in x 11in medium aqua strip. Cross cut this strip set into four segments, 2½in wide.

For Strip Set 4, sew a 2½in x 8½in light aqua strip to either side of the 4½in x 8½in medium aqua strip. Cross cut this strip set into three segments, 2½in wide.

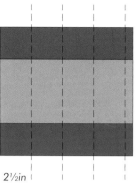

Strip Set 3 – cut 4 segments

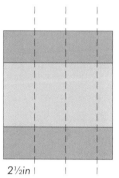

Strip Set 4 – cut 3 segments

2. The segments cut from the strip sets become the center strip of each block. The number of segments indicates the number of blocks to be made in each color combination:

Make six dark grey/red blocks
Make eight light grey/red blocks
Make four red/medium aqua blocks
Make three light aqua/medium aqua blocks.

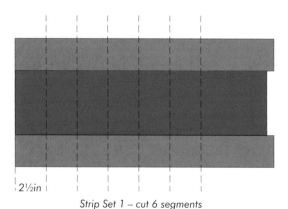

Strip Set 1 – cut 6 segments

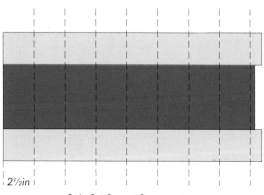

Strip Set 2 – cut 8 segments

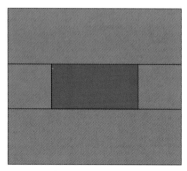

Dark Grey block – make 6

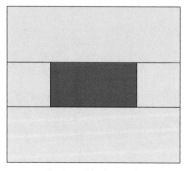

Light Grey block – make 8

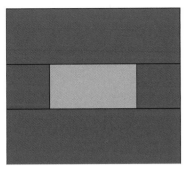

Red block – make 4

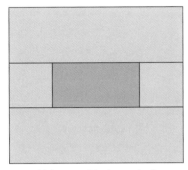

Light aqua block – make 3

3. To make the blocks, sew 2½in x 8½in rectangles the same colour as the end patches in the center strip to either side of the center strip. Press the seams away from the center strip.

JOIN THE BLOCKS

1. Referring to the photograph of the quilt, lay out the blocks in three columns of seven blocks each.
2. The blocks in each column are joined with gently curved seams. Review Freehand Curve Techniques in Quilting Basics on page 89 before you begin to stitch. Start by joining the first two blocks from column 1. Lay the blocks on your work surface, right side up. Align the side edges and overlap the blocks by about 1in.

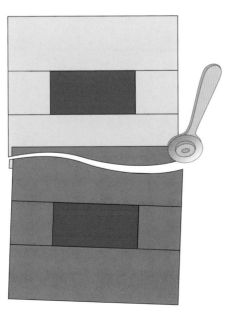

Diagram 1

3. Working freehand, cut a gentle curve line through the overlapped area with a rotary cutter. See Diagram 1. Discard the trimmings.
4. Sew the blocks together. Repeat this process to join all the blocks in the first column. Then join the blocks in the second and third columns together.
5. Because the curves are cut freehand, and each one is slightly different, the three columns of blocks will now be different lengths. From the remaining 2½in strips, cut 8½in rectangles in colors to match the blocks in each column. Cut and sew a rectangle to one or both ends of the columns in the same manner that you used to join the blocks and trim them so that all three columns are the same length.

MAKE THE SASHING STRIPS

1. Join four 1½in strips in the sequence – black and white stripe cut down the length of the fabric (so that the stripes run parallel to the long edges of the strip), red, black and white stripe, medium aqua – to form Strip Set 5. Press all seams in the same direction. Cross cut this strip set into segments 1½in wide.

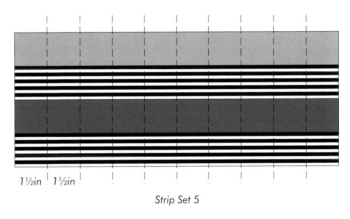

1½in 1½in

Strip Set 5

2. Join the segments to make two pieced strips.

Pieced strips – make 2

3. Measure the length of your columns of blocks, and trim the strips to this length.
4. Sew a pieced strip to one side of each of the 4in red hand dyed strips. Sew the 4in medium aqua hand dyed strip to one pieced strip and the 2½in dark grey hand dyed strip to the other pieced strip to complete Strip Sets 6 and 7. Press seam allowances away from the pieced strips.
5. Referring to the diagram, cut a gentle flowing curve through the center of the red, aqua and dark grey hand dyed strips. This will yield a total of six sashing strips.

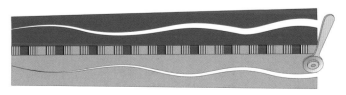

Strip Set 6

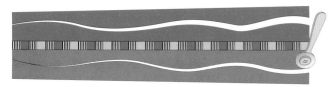

Strip Set 7

ASSEMBLE THE BLOCKS AND SASHING STRIPS

1. Lay out the three columns of blocks and put four of the sashing strips between them and on the outer edges. The curved edge/s on each sashing strip now become the template to cut the curves on the column of blocks to which it will be joined.
2. Lay the center column of blocks and the medium aqua sashing strip right side up on a cutting surface, with the curved side of the sashing strip overlapping the column of blocks. Make sure either the top or the bottom edges of the strips are aligned. Using the curve on the medium aqua sashing as a template, cut the column of blocks along the edge of the curve. Discard the trimmings. It doesn't matter if you cut slightly into the sashing strip, as you will be cutting both fabrics and creating a positive/negative curve. The main aim is to cut as little as possible away from the column of blocks as you cut the curved edge.
3. Sew the sashing to the center column of blocks, starting at the end where the strips were aligned and taking care not to stretch them when matching the raw edges.
4. Sew the right column of blocks to the straight side of the medium aqua sashing strip.
5. Repeat steps 2 and 3 to sew a sashing strip with a pieced strip in its center to the right edge of the right column of blocks and the left edge of the center column of blocks. Then sew the left most column of blocks to the left edge of the sashing strip, and plain red and dark grey sashing strips to the outer edges.
6. Similarly, sew a red strip to the top edge of the quilt and a dark grey strip to the bottom edge of the quilt.

ADD BORDER 1

1. Referring to Adding Borders in Quilting Basics, page 89, measure the length of the quilt. Trim one of the 2½in strips of dark aqua hand dyed fabric to this length and sew it to the left edge of the quilt.
2. Similarly, measure the width of the quilt and trim the remaining 2½in strip of dark aqua hand dyed fabric to this length. Sew it to the top edge of the quilt.
3. Measure the length again, and trim one of the 1½in strips of black and white striped fabric that were cut across the width of the fabric to this length. Sew it to the right edge of the quilt.
4. Measure the length of the quilt and trim the remaining 1½in strip of black and white striped fabric that was cut across the width of the fabric to this length. Sew it to the bottom edge of the quilt.

ADD BORDER 2

1. Referring to Adding Borders in Quilting Basics, page 89, measure the length of the quilt. Trim one of the 6½in strips of precious commercial print fabric to this length. Sew it to the right edge of the quilt.

2. Similarly, measure the width of the quilt. Trim the remaining 6½in strip of precious commercial print fabric to this length. Sew it to the bottom edge of the quilt.
3. Measure the length of the quilt. Trim one of the 2in strips of precious commercial print fabric to this length. Sew it to the left edge of the quilt.
4. Measure the width of the quilt. Trim the remaining 2in strip of precious commercial print fabric to this length. Sew it to the top edge of the quilt.

FINISH THE QUILT

1. Referring to Preparing the Quilt Sandwich in Quilting Basics, page 89, layer the backing, batting and quilt ready for quilting.
2. Quilt as desired. *For the Print* was initially stitched in the ditch around all the blocks and borders using a monofilament thread. This stabilized the quilt. The red and dark grey blocks were then quilted with a triple line of stitching ¼in outside their center rectangles using a thread to contrast with the fabric. The light grey and aqua blocks were quilted with a triple line of stitching ¼in inside their center rectangles using a thread to contrast with the fabric. For Border 3, individual motifs were outlined using free motion stitching worked with monofilament thread.
3. Join the five strips cut for the binding end to end to make one long strip. Use it to bind the quilt, referring to Binding the Quilt in Quilting Basics, page 89.

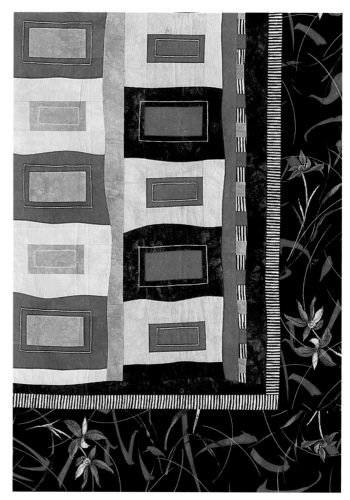

Candy Canes

Designed and made by Gail Simpson
Finished size: 53in x 53in (135cm x 135cm)

Candy Canes

IF YOU LOVE USING UNUSUAL FABRICS, then you will enjoy playing with stripes in this striking quilt. Three easy blocks are repeated with clever color placement in the complex-looking center of the quilt. The setting triangles complement the quilt center without overpowering it.

MATERIALS

2½yd (2.3m) diagonal stripe commercial print fabric
10 hand dyed fat eighths [9in x 21in (25cm x 55cm)]. The colors used in *Candy Canes* as shown are: daffodil, orange, red-orange, pink, rose, red-purple, purple, blue, blue-green and green.
1⅝yd (1.5m) golden yellow hand dyed fabric (background)
3¼yd (2.9m) backing fabric
Batting at least 60in (150cm) square
Neutral thread for sewing
General sewing supplies

CUT THE FABRIC

From the diagonal stripe commercial print fabric, cut:
- 2 strips, 3½in x width of fabric. Cross cut into 16 squares, 3½in (A) (Scot's Plaid blocks).
- 3 strips, 2in x width of fabric. Cross cut into 50 squares, 2in (B) (Scot's Plaid blocks).
- 1 strip, 2in x width of fabric. Cross cut into four rectangles, 2in x 8in (X) (Delectable Mountains blocks).
- 3 strips, 12in x width of fabric. Cross cut into 8 squares, 12in (Y) (setting units).
- 6 strips, 3½in x width of fabric (Border 2)
- 6 strips, 2¼in x width of fabric (binding)

From the golden yellow hand dyed fabric, cut:
- 8 strips, 2in x width of fabric (Borders 1 and 2)
- 2 squares, 19in (setting triangles)
- 8 squares, 8½in (Delectable Mountains blocks)

From the daffodil hand dyed fabric, cut:
- 5 squares, 2in (D) (Scot's Plaid blocks)
- 8 rectangles, 2in x 3½in (E) (Scot's Plaid blocks)

From the orange hand dyed fabric, cut:
- 5 squares, 2in (F) (Scot's Plaid blocks)
- 8 rectangles, 2in x 3½in (G) (Scot's Plaid blocks)

From the red-orange hand dyed fabric, cut:
- 1 square, 8½in (Delectable Mountains blocks)
- 5 squares, 2in (H) (Scot's Plaid blocks)
- 8 rectangles, 2in x 3½in (I) (Scot's Plaid blocks)

From the pink hand dyed fabric, cut:
- 1 square, 8½in (Delectable Mountains blocks)
- 4 squares, 2in (J) (Scot's Plaid blocks)
- 8 rectangles, 2in x 3½in (K) (Scot's Plaid blocks)

From the rose hand dyed fabric, cut:
- 1 square, 8½in (Delectable Mountains blocks)
- 6 squares, 2in (L) (Scot's Plaid blocks)
- 8 rectangles, 2in x 3½in (M) (Scot's Plaid blocks)

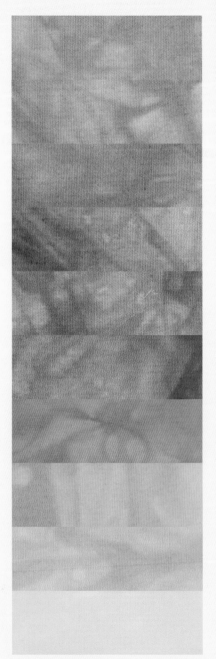

Intermediate

From the red-purple hand dyed fabric, cut:
• 1 square, 8½in (Delectable Mountains blocks)
• 5 squares, 2in (N) (Scot's Plaid blocks)
• 8 rectangles, 2in x 3½in (O) (Scot's Plaid blocks)
From the purple hand-dyed fabric, cut:
• 1 square, 8½in (Delectable Mountains blocks)
• 5 squares, 2in (P) (Scot's Plaid blocks)
• 8 rectangles, 2in x 3½in (Q) (Scot's Plaid blocks)
From the blue hand dyed fabric, cut:
• 1 square, 8½in (Delectable Mountains blocks)
• 5 squares, 2in (R) (Scot's Plaid blocks)
• 8 rectangles, 2in x 3½in (S) (Scot's Plaid blocks)
From the blue-green hand dyed fabric, cut:
• 1 square, 8½in (Delectable Mountains blocks)
• 5 squares, 2in (T) (Scot's Plaid blocks)
• 8 rectangles, 2in x 3½in (U) (Scot's Plaid blocks)
From the green hand dyed fabric, cut:
• 1 square, 8½in (Delectable Mountains blocks)
• 6 squares, 2in (V) (Scot's Plaid blocks)
• 6 rectangles, 2in x 3½in (W) (Scot's Plaid blocks)

MAKE THE SCOT'S PLAID BLOCKS

1. Referring to the diagrams, lay out the patches for each block. Take care to orientate the diagonal stripe A and B squares correctly, so that the stripes run in the direction indicated in the diagrams.

*Block 1 – make 3
(Daffodil/red-purple)*

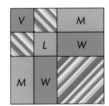

*Block 2 – make 2
(Green/rose)*

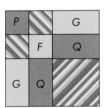

*Block 3 – make 3
(Purple/orange)*

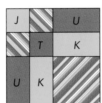

*Block 4 – make 4
(Pink/blue-green)*

*Block 5 – make 3
(Red-orange/blue)*

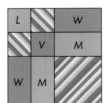

*Block 6 – make 1
(Rose/green)*

2. Each block is made in three rows. Sew the patches in each row together, then sew the three rows together, carefully matching seams. Gently press all seams towards the bottom edge of the block.

If you are working with different colored fabrics from those used in *Candy Canes*, and wish to play with some color options, a line drawing of the blocks in the quilt center is provided on page 51. Photocopying is permitted for personal use.

MAKE THE HALF BLOCKS

1. To carry the design into the border on two sides of the Scot's Plaid blocks, you will need to make eight half blocks. Referring to the diagrams, lay out the patches for each half block. Again, take care to orientate the diagonal stripe A and B squares correctly, so that the stripes run in the direction indicated in the diagrams.

Half Block 1 – make 1 and 1 reversed (Red-orange/blue)

Half Block 2 – make 1 and 1 reversed (Daffodil/red-purple)

Half Block 3 – make 1 and 1 reversed (Rose/green)

Half Block 4 – make 1 and 1 reversed (Purple/orange)

2. Each block is made from two rows. Sew the patches in each row together, then sew the two rows together, carefully matching seams. Gently press all seams towards the bottom edge of the block.
3. The final block for the quilt center is a Four-patch. Refer to the diagram and make one.

Four-patch – make 1

ASSEMBLE THE QUILT CENTER

1. Referring to the Quilt Layout Diagram, lay out the 16 Scot's Plaid blocks, the eight Half Blocks, and the Four-patch block. The diagonal stripes on the large squares should all lie in one direction, while the stripes on the small squares should all lie in the other.
2. Sew each row of blocks together. Then sew the rows together, carefully matching seams. Press seams to one side.
3. Referring to Adding Borders in Quilting Basics page 89, measure the quilt vertically. Trim two of the 2in strips of golden yellow hand dyed fabric to this length. Sew them to the left and right edges of the quilt.
4. In the same manner, measure the quilt horizontally. Trim two of the 2in strips of golden yellow hand dyed fabric to this length.

Quilt Layout Diagram

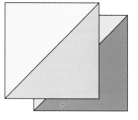
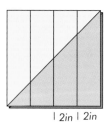

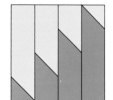
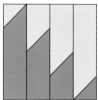

Diagram 2

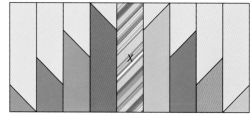

Delectable Mountains blocks – make 16 (8 of each kind)

Sew them to the top and bottom edges of the quilt to complete the quilt center. Your quilt should now measure 30½in square from raw edge to raw edge.

MAKE THE DELECTABLE MOUNTAINS BLOCKS

1. Draw a diagonal line on the wrong side of each of the eight 8½in squares of golden yellow hand dyed fabric.
2. Match one of these golden yellow squares with the 8½in square of green hand dyed fabric, right sides together. Sew ¼in on either side of the diagonal line.
3. Cut on the diagonal line and press the seams towards the hand dyed fabric. You will now have two half-square triangle blocks. See Diagram 1.

Diagram 1

4. Trim to measure 8in square with the seam running through two corners.
5. Match these two squares right sides together as shown in Diagram 2. This will ensure that you create half of your Delectable Mountains blocks in reverse. Cut them into four 2in segments.
6. Lay out the segments, right side up, into two Delectable Mountains blocks – one is the reverse of the other. See diagram.
7. Repeat these steps, pairing each of the golden yellow squares with a hand dyed 8½in square to yield a total of 16 Delectable Mountains blocks. This is more blocks than are needed to make

the quilt. However, making more will give you the full range of color choices as you assemble the blocks for your quilt.
8. The next step is to rearrange the segments so that each segment in a Delectable Mountains block is a different color. Because you have made more Delectable Mountains blocks than you need, you can mix and match segments and arrange the colors in whatever order appeals to you. Following the process described in step 9 below is just one way to achieve this.
9. Stack four Delectable Mountain blocks of the same kind (all reverse blocks or all not-reversed blocks) on top of each other, all facing right side up. Leave the stack of #1 segments as is. Lift one #2 segment off the top of the stack of #2 segments and put it on the bottom of that stack. Lift two #3 segments off the top of the stack of #3 segments and put them at the bottom of that stack. Move the #4 segment at the bottom of the stack of #4 segments and put it on the top of that stack.
10. Once you have arranged segments for four Delectable Mountains blocks and four reversed Delectable Mountains blocks in a way that appeals to you, sew the segments in each block together along their long edges.
11. Lay out a Delectable Mountains block and a reversed Delectable Mountains block. Put an X striped rectangle between them. Join the blocks to its left and right edges. Repeat to make four units like this. See Diagram 3.

Diagram 3

COMPLETE THE SETTING UNITS

1. Mark the centers of each side of the Y stripe squares. Cut from one mark to another, as shown in Diagram 4, to yield eight squares with the printed stripes running parallel to two edges. Handle these squares carefully as you work with them, because their edges are cut on the bias.

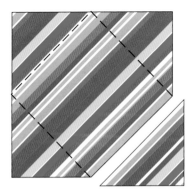

Diagram 4

2. Sew a square to each end of the Delectable Mountains units. Repeat to make four setting units. Press all seams towards the edges.

3. Cut each of the 19in golden yellow hand dyed squares along one diagonal. Sew each of the triangles to the top edge of the setting units. Before sewing, make sure the tip of the triangle is aligned with the center of the X strip. See Diagram 4.

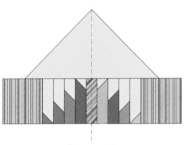

Diagram 4

4. Place a ruler on the edge of the golden yellow triangle and trim the striped square, as shown in the diagram below. Repeat at the other end of the setting unit. Repeat with all the setting units.

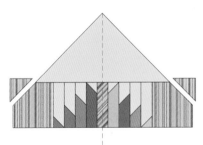

Trimming the setting units

5. Mark the middle of each X strip. Mark the middle of each side of the quilt center. Matching these points, pin, then sew a setting unit to two opposite sides of the quilt.

6. Repeat to sew the remaining two setting units to the other sides of the quilt.

7. The setting units have been made slightly over-size. Trim them so that they are even with the edges of the golden yellow corner triangles.

ADD THE BORDERS

1. Join the remaining 2in golden yellow strips end to end to make one long strip.

2. Referring to Adding Borders in Quilting Basics, page 89, measure the quilt vertically. Trim two strips this length from the long strip and sew them to the left and right edges of the quilt.

3. In the same way, measure the quilt horizontally. Trim two strips this length from the long strip and sew them to the top and bottom edges of the quilt. Press seams towards the border.

4. Join the 3½in diagonal stripe strips to make one long strip.

5. Repeat steps 2 and 3 to add Border 2 to the quilt.

FINISH THE QUILT

1. Cut the length of backing fabric in half. Remove the selvages. Join the two sections together down a long edge, then trim to 57in square for the backing of the quilt.

2. Referring to Preparing the Quilt Sandwich in Quilting Basics, page 89, layer the backing, batting and quilt ready for quilting. Thread or pin-baste.

3. Quilt as desired. *Candy Canes* was machine quilted with outlines of the Delectable Mountains block in the golden yellow setting triangles, and a large meander elsewhere.

4. Join the six strips cut for the binding end to end to make one long strip. Use it to bind the quilt, referring to Binding the Quilt in Quilting Basics, page 89.

Use this diagram to explore color options for your own Candy Canes quilt.

Kites Afloat

HAND DYED FABRICS often solve the dilemma of what to do with a precious fabric. I purchased the background fabric for Kites Afloat *with no idea how I would use it. After more than a year of just looking at it, I started making Kaleidoscope blocks, using the precious print as the background. The print – which looks like it has sequins all over it – provided the perfect foil for the hand dyed fabrics.*

MATERIALS

12 hand dyed fat eighths [9in x 21in (25cm x 55cm)] grouped in four sets of three colors each. In *Kites Afloat* yellow/light orange/dark orange; red/pink/purple; dark purple/dark blue/mid blue and dark green/mid green/yellow green were used.

Fat quarter each of two contrasting hand dyed fabrics (corner triangles). In *Kites Afloat,* orange and blue were used.

2yd (1.8m) multicolored 'sequin' commercial print fabric

3yd (2.7m) backing fabric

Batting at least 50in x 63in (126cm x 159cm)

Nifty Notions 45 degree Kaleidoscope Ruler or Template A made using the shape on page 55

Template plastic and black permanent marking pen (if making a template)

Neutral sewing thread

Rotary cutter, ruler and mat

Sewing machine and general sewing supplies

CUT THE FABRIC

From each of the 12 fat eighths of hand dyed fabrics, cut:
• Two strips, 2½in x length of fat eighth (21in)

From each of the orange and blue hand dyed fabrics, cut:
• 12 squares, 4in. Cross cut each square once on the diagonal to yield 24 half-square triangles.

From the multicolored sequin commercial print fabric, cut:
• Two strips, 6½in x width of fabric. Cross cut into 48 triangles using the Kaleidoscope Ruler or Template A.
• Five strips, 4½in x width of fabric (border)
• Six strips, 2½in x width of fabric (sashing)
• Six strips, 2¼in x width of fabric (binding)

MAKE THE BLOCKS

1. Join a yellow, orange and dark orange 2½in strip together along their long edges to form Strip Set 1. Make 2.

Strip Set 1 – make 2

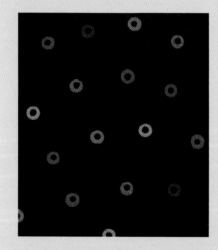

Intermediate

Designed and made by Gail Simpson; quilted by Kim Bradley
Finished size: 45½in x 58½in (115.5cm x 148.5cm)
Block size: 11in (28in)

2. Repeat this process for each of the remaining three groups of hand dyed strips. Make 2 strip sets for each color group (see diagrams). Press all seams in one direction.

Strip Set 2 – make 2

Strip Set 3 – make 2

Strip Set 4 – make 2

3. Align the Kaleidoscope Ruler or Template A with the bottom edge of Strip Set 1. If you are using the Ruler, you will need to match the horizontal line at 6½in with the edge of the strip set. Cut 12 yellow/orange/dark orange kaleidoscope triangles. See Diagram 1.

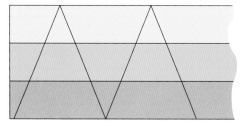

Diagram 1

4. Repeat for each strip set to yield a total of 48 triangles.
5. Sew an orange half-square triangle to each of the triangles cut from the green and blue strip sets. See Diagram 2. Sew a blue half-square triangle to each of the triangle cut from the pink and yellow strip sets. Press the seams towards the half-square triangles.
5. For each Kaleidoscope block, lay out one triangle cut from each of the four different strip sets and four multicolor sequin triangles. Sew a multicolored sequin triangle to the right edge of each hand dyed triangle to form quarter Kaleidoscope units. See Diagram 3.

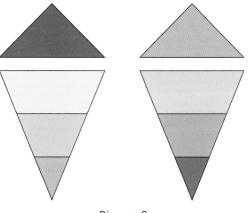

Diagram 2

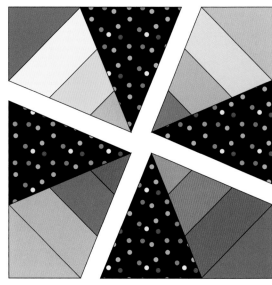

Diagram 3

6. Pair the quarter Kaleidoscope units and join them together to make half blocks. Finger press the seams open.
7. Sew two half blocks together to form a complete Kaleidoscope block. Repeat to make 12 blocks. They should measure 11½in from raw edge to raw edge.

Kaleidoscope block – make 12

ASSEMBLE THE QUILT

1. Using the color photograph of *Kites Afloat* as a guide, lay out the blocks in three columns of four blocks each.
2. Cross cut three of the 2½in strips of multicolored sequin print into nine rectangles, 2½in x 11½in. Lay them horizontally between the blocks in each column.
3. Stitch the blocks and sashing strips in each column together. Press the seams towards the sashings.
4. Join the remaining three 2½in strips of multicolored sequin print end to end to make one long strip. Measure the length of the columns and cut two strips this length from the long strip.
5. Sew the three columns together with a long sashing strip between columns.

ADD THE BORDER

1. Join the five 4½in strips of multicolored sequin print together end to end to make one long strip. Referring to Adding Borders in Quilting Basics, page 89, measure the length of the quilt. Cut two strips this length from the long strip. Sew them to the left and right edges of the quilt.
2. In the same way, measure the width of the quilt. Cut two strips this length from the remainder of the long strip. Sew them to the top and bottom edges of the quilt. Press the seams towards the border.

FINISH THE QUILT

1. Cut the length of backing fabric in half. Remove the selvages. Referring to Piecing the Backing in Quilting Basics, page 89, join the two sections and trim to 50in x 63in for the backing of the quilt.
2. Referring to Preparing the Quilt Sandwich in Quilting Basics, page 89, layer the backing, batting and quilt ready for quilting.
3. Quilt as desired. *Kites Afloat* was machine quilted by Kim Bradley. She worked an overall repeating curvelinear design in multicolored thread.
4. Join the six strips cut for the binding end to end to make one long strip. Use it to bind the quilt, referring to Binding the Quilt in Quilting Basics, page 89.

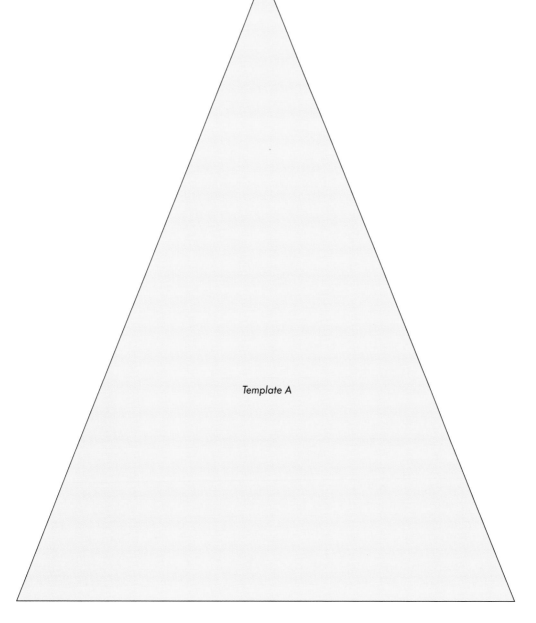

Template A

Almost Country

THE COLOR WHEEL BLOCK in this quilt is my original block design, created specifically to showcase this range of hand dyed fabrics. I was so pleased with the way it worked I decided to create a quilt from the block. Set on point, this quilt would also make a stunning centerpiece for a larger medallion quilt.

MATERIALS

12 hand dyed fat eighths [9in x 21in (25cm x 55cm)]. In *Almost Country* the colors used were: mustard, ochre, burnt orange, brown orange, scarlet, russet, grape, plum, navy, blue green, moss green and yellow green.
One extra 10in (25cm) square of a mid green hand dyed fabric (stems in the center appliquéd block)
2yd (1.8m) light commercial print fabric (background)
1yd (90cm) multicolored commercial print (appliqué, peeper strips, border and binding)
2⅞yd (2.6m) backing fabric
Batting at least 57in (142cm) square
20in (50cm) square of fusible web
Neutral thread for piecing
Rayon thread to match appliqué fabrics
HB pencil
Rotary cutter, ruler and mat
Sewing machine and general sewing supplies

CUT THE FABRIC

From each of the 12 hand dyed fabrics, cut:
• Four rectangles, 2in x 10in (Color Wheel blocks)
• Two strips, 1½in x 6½in (Border 1)
From the light commercial print fabric, cut:
• One strip, 14in x width of fabric. Cross cut one rectangle, 13in x 14in (center block). From the remaining piece, cut four rectangles, 3½in x 24½in (Color Wheel blocks).
• One strip, 6in x width of fabric. Cross cut into 21 rectangles, 2in x 6in (Color Wheel blocks).
• One strip, 4½in x width of fabric. Cross cut into 21 rectangles, 2in x 4½in (Color Wheel blocks).
• One strip, 2in x width of fabric. Cross cut into three rectangles, 2in x 6in and three rectangles, 2in x 4½in (Color Wheel blocks).
• Four squares, 7in (appliquéd Border 1 corner blocks)
• Three strips, 8in x width of fabric. Cross cut into 48 rectangles, 2½in x 8in (Border 1 setting segments)
• Two strips, 6½in x width of fabric. Cross cut into 32 rectangles, 1½in x 6½in (Border 1). From the remaining piece, cut four squares, 4½in. Cross cut each square once on the diagonal to yield eight half-square triangles (Border 1 corner segments).
From the multicolored commercial print, cut:
• Four strips, 1in x 24½in (peeper strips)
• Four squares, 1½in
• Five strips, 2½in x width of fabric (Border 2)
• Six strips, 2¼in x width of fabric (binding)
Set aside the rest of the fabric for appliqué.

Advanced ☐ ☐ ☐

Designed and made by Gail Simpson
Finished size: 52in (132cm) square

APPLIQUÉ THE CENTER BLOCK

Instructions are provided for appliqué using fusible web and buttonhole stitch. But the design lends itself to a variety of appliqué techniques. Adapt the instructions for the appliqué method of your choice.

One of the bonuses of working with hand dyed fabrics is that there is no right or wrong side of the fabric. Just choose the side you prefer.

1. Trace the shapes for the pot, flowers and leaves from page 61 onto the paper side of the fusible web. You will need to trace one pot, one large flower, two small flowers, one large flower center, two small flower centers, two small leaves and one large leaf. The shapes for the leaves have been printed in reverse to assist you. Leave at least ½in between shapes. Cut the shapes out about ¼in outside the traced lines.

2. For the stems, draw one rectangle ⅜in x 8½in and two rectangles ⅜in x 6in on to the paper side of the fusible web. Cut them out ¼in outside the lines.

3. Iron the fusible web shapes onto the wrong side of the following fabrics:

- pot: multicolored commercial print fabric.
- stems: extra 10in (25cm) square of green hand dyed fabric. Because you will be curving the stems a little, it is important to fuse the rectangles for them on the bias of this fabric.
- leaves: green hand dyed fabrics left after cutting strips for the Color Wheel blocks.
- petals and flower centers: red/orange hand dyed fabrics left after cutting strips for the Color Wheel blocks

4. Trim the 13in x 14in light background rectangle to 13in square. Using the quilt photograph and Center Block Layout diagram as a guide, arrange the shapes for the flowers, stems, leaves and pot. Match the bottom edge of the pot with the bottom edge of the background square. Keep the other shapes at least

Center Block Layout

1in from the raw edges of the block. Slip the base of the stems under the top edge of the pot and the leaf ends under the stems.

5. Remove the paper backing from the leaves and stems and fuse them into place. Curve the bias stems a little as you fuse them. Using your preferred appliqué method and thread of choice, sew along both sides of each stem and around the leaves. Using a straight stitch, stitch a few veins in each leaf.

6. Remove the paper backing from the pot and the flowers and fuse in place. Stitch around the edges of these shapes. There is no need to stitch the bottom edge of the pot, as it will be caught in the seam. Fuse a flower center on each flower and stitch in place.

7. To decorate the flowers, add some freehand stitching or a few hand stitched French knots.

8. Press the block and trim it to 12½in square.

APPLIQUÉ THE CORNER BLOCKS

1. Draw four rectangles ⅜in x 4in on the paper side of the fusible web for the stems. Trace the shapes for the corner flowers and leaves from page 61 onto the paper side of the fusible web. You will need to trace four double leaves, four upper petals, four lower petals and four small flower centers. Leave at least ½in between shapes. Cut the shapes out about ¼in outside the traced lines.

2. Iron the fusible web shapes onto the wrong side of the following fabrics:

- stems: multicolored commercial print fabric. Note that the rectangles for these stems do not need to be fused on the bias of the fabric.
- leaves: green hand dyed fabric
- petals and flower centers: red/orange hand dyed fabrics left after cutting strips for the Color Wheel blocks

3. Using the Corner Block Layout and the quilt photograph as a guide, arrange a flower, stem and leaves across the diagonal of each of the 7in squares of light commercial print fabric. One end of the stems should overlap the corner of the background square. Appliqué the shapes in place. Begin with the stem, then the leaves, the upper petals, the flower center and finally the lower petals. The lower petals cover the edges of the stems, leaf ends, the upper petals and flower center.

4. Trim the blocks to 6½in square.

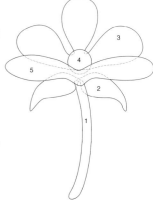

Corner Block Layout

MAKE THE COLOR WHEEL BLOCKS

1. Lay out one 2in x 10in strip of each of the 12 hand dyed fabrics in six rows of two strips each. Refer to the photograph for guidance with color placement; mix and match your strips until

you have an array that you like. The blocks in *Almost Country* have warmer colors at one end of the block and cooler colors at the other.

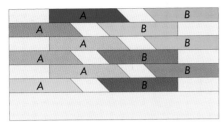

Color Wheel Block Diagram

2. Sew a 2in x 4½in strip of light commercial print fabric to each of the six hand dyed strips marked A in the Color Wheel Block Layout Diagram. To do this, lay the light commercial print rectangle at right angles on the right end of the strip of hand dyed fabric, raw edges matching and right sides together. See Diagram 2. Draw

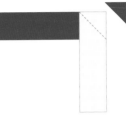

Diagram 2

a line at 45 degrees across the end of the light commercial rectangle, and sew on the line. Turn the strips over and trim the hand dyed fabric only, ¼in away from the stitching. Keeping the light commercial print fabric rectangle intact maintains the shape of the strip, preventing distortion.

3. Turn the strips back over and fold the background fabric up and over, so that it is parallel to the hand dyed strip. Finger press only at this stage to avoid distorting the fabrics.

4. Sew the hand dyed strips marked B in the Color Wheel Block Diagram to the other end of the light commercial fabric rectangle, using the same method. Again, trim only the hand dyed corner, then finger press the hand dyed strip up and over to form a strip. The back of the strips should look like Diagram 3.

Diagram 3 – back of the pieced strips

5. Repeat to make six strips for each Color Wheel block.

6. Lay out the strips for a block in your preferred sequence, off-setting alternate strip as shown in the Block Diagram above. Sew a 2in x 6in rectangle of light commercial print fabric in place at one end of each strip row. In rows 1, 3 and 5, these rectangles will be sewn to the left edge of the strips; in rows 2, 4 and 6, these rectangles will be sewn to the right edge of the strips.

7. Once the strips for a block have been completed, sew them together along their long edges.

8. Measure the length of each block. If your blocks are slightly longer than 24½in, you will need to trim them. Trim the same amount from each end of the block. Ensure that your blocks are straight and the corners are 90 degree angles.

9. Sew a 3½in x 24½in strip of light commercial print fabric to the bottom edge of each Color Wheel block. The blocks should now measure 12½in x 24½in from raw edge to raw edge.

ADD THE PEEPER STRIPS

1. A peeper strip is a folded flap of fabric, stitched into the seam between fabric patches. The folded edge of the strip is not sewn down. Fold a 1in x 24½in strip of multicolored commercial print fabric in half, long edges matching and wrong sides together. Press.

Tip

It is very important that the peeper strip is the same length as the Color Wheel block or even a tiny little bit longer and then trimmed to size. It must not be any shorter than the block and stretched to size, as this will cause the block to become distorted.

2. Match the raw edges of the folded peeper strip with the raw edges of the 3½in strip of light commercial print fabric on the bottom edge of the Color Wheel block. Stitch in place with a seam allowance of just over ⅛in. This narrow seam ⅛in ensures that this stitching is hidden when the blocks are sewn together.

3. Press the block, being careful not to stretch the top edge where the short light commercial print patch has a bias edge.

4. Repeat with the remaining Color Wheel blocks.

ASSEMBLE THE QUILT

1. The quilt center is the appliquéd block surrounded by four rectangular Color Wheel blocks. Place the center appliqué block on your design wall or work surface. Lay out the four Color Wheel blocks around it, referring to the Quilt Layout Diagram and the quilt photograph for guidance.

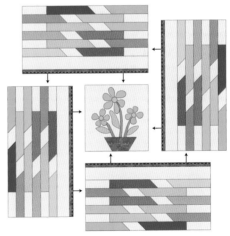

Quilt Layout Diagram

2. Start assembling the quilt by stitching a Color Wheel block to the top edge of the appliquéd center block. The peeper strip should be sandwiched between the appliquéd block and the Color Wheel block. Use a partial seam only at this stage; that is, only stitch about 8in along the top of the appliquéd block, leaving the rest of the seam unstitched. See Diagram 4. The stitches that hold the peeper strip to the Color Wheel block should be hidden as you work this seam.

3. Next, stitch another Color Wheel block to the center square and the short edge of the first Color Wheel block. Press the

seam towards the second Color Wheel block.

4. In a similar manner join the third and fourth Color Wheel blocks to the center.

5. Finally, return to the first seam that you sewed between the first Color Wheel Block and the center square. You can now complete the stitching, joining this Color Wheel block to the top edge of the center square and

Diagram 4

the short end of the fourth Color Wheel block. Your quilt should now measure 36½in square.

ADD BORDER 1

1. Join a 1½in x 6½in rectangle of light commercial print fabric to either side of a 1½in square of multicolored commercial print fabric. See diagram. This is the center unit for each Border 1 strip. Make 4.

Center unit – make 4

2. Stitch a 1½in x 6½in rectangle of light commercial print fabric to each 1½in x 6½in rectangle of hand dyed fabric along their long edges. Cut each of these strip sets into 1½in segments, as shown in Diagram 5.

1½in

Diagram 5

3. Lay out the segments cut from these strips in eight rows. Each row will have one square of each hand dyed fabric in it. The segments should be laid out so that the hand dyed fabrics are in the same order as they are in the Color Wheel blocks.

4. Join adjacent pairs of squares together to make Four-patch blocks. See Diagram 6. Place the blocks back in the layout in the correct position. Repeat with all the pairs of squares.

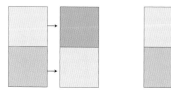

Diagram 6

5. On one of the 2½in x 8in light commercial print rectangles, measure 2¾in down from the top right corner and mark with a pencil on the right side of the fabric. Then measure up 2¾in from the bottom left corner and mark with a pencil. Draw a line to connect the points, as shown in Diagram 7.

5. Stack three 2½in x 8in light commercial print fabric rectangles on top of each other, right side up. Place the rectangle you marked in step 4 on top, also right side up. Cross cut the stack of rectangles on the drawn line.

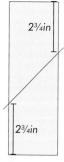

2¾in

2¾in

Diagram 7

6. Repeat with the remaining light commercial print rectangles – 11 stacks of four rectangles – to yield a total of 96 setting segments.

7. Referring to Diagram 8, join a setting segment to two opposite sides of every Four-patch block. Place each unit back in the correct position in your layout.

8. Referring to Diagram 9, and being careful to maintain the correct color sequence, sew together the units in each border strip: six units, a center unit, and then another six units, reversing the color sequence. Stitch a light commercial print 4½in half-square triangle to each end of the strip.

Diagram 8

Diagram 9

7. Trim the center unit on each Border 1 strip even with the edges of the other units. Do not iron the border strips at this stage: they have bias edges and need to be secured to prevent stretching. Using a long running stitch, stay stitch along both sides of the strips about ½in from the edge, taking care not to stretch the edges. Then gently press and trim each strip to 6½in x 36½in.

8. Referring to Adding Borders in Quilting Basics, page 89, pin, then sew a Border 1 strip to the left and right edges of the quilt. Press the seams outwards.

9. Join a corner appliqué block to each end of the remaining two Border 1 strips. Pin, then sew these Border 1 strips to the top and bottom edges of the quilt. Press as before.

ADD BORDER 2

1. Join the 2½in strips of multicolored commercial print fabric end to end to make one long strip.

2. Referring to Adding Borders in Quilting Basics, page 89, measure the quilt vertically and trim two strips this length from the long strip. Sew them to the left and right edges of the quilt. Press seams towards the border strips.

3. Measure the quilt horizontally, and trim two strips this length from the long strip. Sew the strips to the top and bottom edges of the quilt.

4. Remove any visible stay stitching.

FINISH THE QUILT

1. Referring to Piecing the Backing in Quilting, page 89, cut the length of backing fabric in half. Remove the selvages. Join the two sections together, then trim to 57in square for the backing of the quilt.

2. Referring to Preparing the Quilt Sandwich in Quilting Basics, page 89, layer the backing, batting and quilt ready for quilting.

3. Quilt as desired. *Almost Country* was machine quilted on a long arm machine by Kaye Brown. She outlined the appliqué shapes, worked a loopy meander on the light commercial print background and the outer border, and left the hand dyed fabrics unquilted.

4. Join the six strips cut for the binding end to end to make one long strip. Use it to bind the quilt, referring to Binding the Quilt in Quilting Basics, page 89.

Shapes have been printed in reverse for tracing on to fusible web.

Small flower center – trace 10

Large flower – trace 1

Small flower – trace 2

Upper petals – trace 4

Double leaves – trace 4

Large flower center – trace 1

Lower petals – trace 4

Large leaf – trace 1

Small leaf #2 – trace 1

Pot – trace 1

Small leaf #1 – trace 1

NewStar on the Block

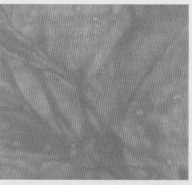

THIS QUILT IS A GREAT WAY TO DISPLAY LARGE PIECES of hand dyed fabric with a collection of black and whites prints. Put them together with a dark background and you have a sensational quilt that will be the envy of all. The large stars are easy to make by breaking the block down into smaller units. A small Nine-patch block forms the center of each of the smaller stars and the points are made with connectors stitched to the sashing strips and the pieced border.

MATERIALS

½yd (50cm) lime hand dyed fabric
⅝yd (60cm) pink hand dyed fabric
3¼yd (3m) dark hand dyed or commercial print fabric
9 fat eighths [9in x 21in (25cm x 55cm)] black and white commercial print fabrics
4yd (3.6m) backing fabric
Batting at least 69in (175cm) square
Rotary cutter, ruler and mat
Neutral thread for piecing
Sewing machine
General sewing supplies

CUT THE FABRIC

From the lime hand dyed fabric, cut:
• One strip, 3in x width of fabric. Cross cut into 14 squares, 3in (B) (Unit 1).
• One strip, 4in x width of fabric. Cross cut into four squares, 4in (C) (Unit 1). Trim the remaining strip to cut two squares, 3in (B) (Unit 1) and four squares, 1½in (I) (Unit 3).
• One strip, 2½in x width of fabric. Cross cut into 16 squares, 2½in (H) (Unit 3).
• One strip, 6½in x width of fabric. Cross cut into five rectangles, 1½in x 6½in (strip sets). Trim the remaining piece of this strip to 6¼in wide and from it, cross cut four squares, 6¼in (F) (Unit 2).

From the pink hand dyed fabric, cut:
• One strip, 3in x width of fabric. Cross cut into 14 squares, 3in (B) (Unit 1).
• One strip, 4in x width of fabric. Cross cut into four squares, 4in (C) (Unit 1). Trim the remaining strip to cut six squares, 3in (B) (Unit 1) and four squares, 1½in (I) (Unit 3).
• One strip, 2½in x width of fabric. Cross cut into 16 squares, 2½in (H) (Unit 3).
• One strip, 6¼in x width of fabric. Cross cut into five squares, 6¼in (F) (Unit 2).
• Three strips, 1½in x width of fabric. Cross cut into five rectangles, 1½in x 19in (strip sets).

From the dark hand dyed or commercial print fabric, cut:
• Three strips, 4in x width of fabric. Cross cut into 36 rectangles, 3in x 4in (A) (Unit 1).
• One strip, 6¼in x width of fabric. Cross cut into six squares, 6¼in (E) (Unit 2).
• One strip, 6¼in x width of fabric. Cross cut into three squares, 6¼in (E) (Unit 2). Cut the remaining piece of this strip into four 1½in strips and from these, cross cut into 36 rectangles, 1½in x 2½in (G) (Unit 3).

Advanced ▯ ▯ ▯

Designed by Gail Simpson; patchwork by Fay Winther; quilted by Rhonda Coates
Finished size: 65in x 65in (165cm x 165cm)
Block size: NewStar blocks: 13in   Nine-patch blocks: 3in

• Three strips, 1½in x width of fabric. Cross cut one strip into four rectangles, 1½in x 6½in (strip sets); cross cut the other two strips into four rectangles, 1½in x 19in (strip sets).
• Two strips, 13½in x width of fabric. Cross cut into 24 rectangles, 3½in x 13½in (sashing).
• Two strips, 3½in x width of fabric. Cross cut into 20 squares, 3½in (K) (extra star points and sashing corners).
• Seven strips, 4½in x width of fabric (border)
• Seven strips, 2¼in x width of fabric (binding)
From each of the nine black and white prints, cut:
• Two squares, 6¼in (D)
• 16 squares, 2⅛in (J). Note: only 128 squares are required for this project. Having some extras will allow you to play with the placement of different prints.

MAKE THE BLOCK CORNERS (UNIT 1)

1. Referring to Diagram 1, lay out four dark background A rectangles, four lime B squares and one lime C square in three rows of three patches.

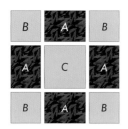

Diagram 1

2. Join the patches in each row together, then join the rows together, carefully matching seams. Press gently.
3. Repeat steps 1 – 2 to make four lime and five pink blocks like this.
4. Cut through the center of the blocks both vertically and horizontally as shown in Diagram 2. Each block will yield four 4½in squares for Unit 1, which are the corners of the NewStar Block. You will have a total of 16 lime Unit 1 and 20 pink Unit 1.

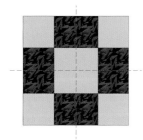

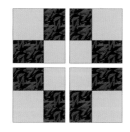

Diagram 2

MAKE THE STAR POINTS (UNIT 2)

1. Draw a diagonal line on the back of each black and white D square.
2. Match nine of the D squares with dark background E squares, right sides together. Match the remaining nine D squares with lime or pink F squares, right sides together. Sew a ¼in either side of the drawn line. Cut along the drawn line, open out the pieced squares and press seams towards the darker fabric. You will have 18 dark background/black and white pieced squares, eight lime/black and white pieced squares and 10 pink/black and white pieced squares.

Background pieced squares – make 18   *Lime pieced squares – make 8*   *Pink pieced squares – make 10*

3. Match each lime and pink pieced square with a background pieced square, right sides together. Make sure that the black and white print triangles are on opposite sides of the squares, not on top of each other. Draw a diagonal line on the back of the top square perpendicular to the seam. See Diagram 3.

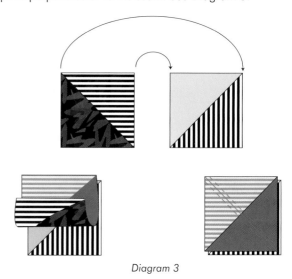

Diagram 3

4. Sew a ¼in either side of this drawn line. Cut along the drawn line and open out the pieced squares. Press. They should measure 5½in from raw edge to raw edge.
5. Trim each square across the hand dyed edge as shown in the diagrams to yield a Unit 2, 4½in x 5½in. Make 16 lime Unit 2 and 20 pink Unit 2.

Lime and background pieced squares – make 16   *Pink and background pieced squares – make 20*

MAKE THE STAR CENTERS (UNIT 3)

1. Referring to Diagram 4, lay out four dark background G rectangles, four lime H squares and one lime I square.

Diagram 4

2. Join the patches in each row together, then join the rows together, carefully matching seams. Press gently.

3. Repeat steps 1 – 2 to make nine Unit 3, four with lime H and I squares and five with pink H and I squares.

ASSEMBLE THE NEWSTAR BLOCKS

1. Referring to the Block Diagram, lay out four lime Unit 1, four lime Unit 2 and one lime Unit 3 in three rows of three patches each. Double check that you have orientated the Unit 1 and Unit 2 correctly before you begin sewing.

2. Sew the Units together in rows, then sew the rows together, carefully matching seams. The block should measure 13½in square, from raw edge to raw edge.

3. Repeat steps 1 – 2 to make four lime NewStar blocks and five pink NewStar blocks.

NewStar Block Diagram

MAKE THE NINE-PATCH BLOCKS

1. The sashings between the blocks are made from small Nine-patch blocks and connector strips. To make the small Nine-patch blocks, start by piecing strip sets.

2. Stitch the 1½in x 6½in strips of dark background fabric to the 1½in x 6½in strips of lime hand dyed fabric to make two Strip Set A and one Strip Set B.

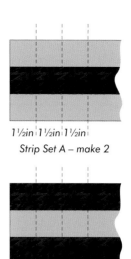

1½in 1½in 1½in
Strip Set A – make 2

1½in 1½in 1½in
Strip Set B – make 1

3. Cross cut the strip sets into 1½in segments. Cut four segments from each strip. (The strip sets are a little longer than needed to allow for straightening up as you cut.)

4. Stitch the 1½in x 19in strips of dark background fabric to the 1½in x 19in strips of pink hand dyed fabric to make two Strip Set C and one Strip Set D.

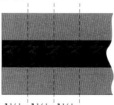

1½in 1½in 1½in
Strip Set C – make 2

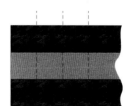

1½in 1½in 1½in
Strip Set D – make 1

5. Cross cut the strip sets into 1½in segments. Cut 12 segments from each strip. (The strip sets are a little longer than needed to allow for straightening up as you cut.)

6. To make the lime Nine-patch blocks, lay out one Strip Set B segment between two Strip Set A segments. Sew the segments together, carefully matching seams. The block should measure 3½in from raw edge to raw edge. Repeat to make four lime Nine-patch blocks.

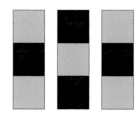

Nine-patch block: make 4 lime and 12 pink

7. To make the pink Nine-patch blocks, lay out one Strip Set D segment between two Strip Set C segments. Sew the segments together, carefully matching seams. Repeat to make 12 pink Nine-patch blocks.

MAKE THE CONNECTOR SASHINGS

1. Referring to Connectors in Quilting Basics, page 89, sew two J squares cut from the same black and white print fabric to one end of the 24 background sashing strips. The J squares have been cut a tiny little bit oversized to ensure that they meet in the center of the strip.

2. Repeat to sew two J squares cut from another black and white print to the other end of each sashing strip.

Connector sashings – make 24

3. You may choose your J squares at random to give a scrappy look or plan ahead, as Gail has done, so that when the sashings are laid out with the Nine-patch blocks, each Nine-patch star will have star points made from the same black and white print.

MAKE THE EXTRA STAR POINTS

1. Referring to Connectors in Quilting Basics, page 89, sew two J squares cut from the same black and white print fabric to one edge of a K background square to form a star point.

Star point – make 16

2. Repeat to make 16 star points like this.

ASSEMBLE THE QUILT CORNERS

1. There a numerous ways to go about assembling all the units, blocks and sashings for the quilt. Gail prefers to avoid making long narrow strips and then sewing them together. She prefers to assemble square-ish units and then stitch them together.

Sashing corner unit

2. Lay out one pink Nine-patch block, one background K square and two extra star points in two rows of two patches each. Join the patches in each row together, then join the rows to make a sashing corner unit.

3. Lay out a dark background 3½in x 13in rectangle, a connector sashing, a pink nine-patch block and a star point block in two rows of two patches each. Join the patches in each row together, then join the rows to make a sashing side unit.

Sashing side unit - right

4. Repeat to make another sashing side unit, this time with the nine-patch and star point block at the other end.

Sashing side unit – left

5. Referring to the Quilt Corner Assembly Diagram, lay out a pink NewStar block, a sashing corner unit, a sashing side unit (right), a sashing side unit (left), two connector sashings and a lime Nine-patch block.

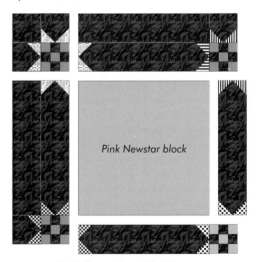

Quilt Corner Assembly Diagram

6. Stitch a connector sashing to the right edge of the NewStar block. Stitch the lime Nine-patch to one end of the other connector sashing, then stitch this unit to the bottom edge of the NewStar block. Stitch the sashing side unit (left) to the left edge of the block. Join the sashing corner unit to the sashing side unit (right), then join them to the top of the block.

7. Repeat steps 1 – 6 to make the four corners of the quilt.

ASSEMBLE THE QUILT SIDES

1. Referring to the Quilt Side Assembly Diagram, lay out two connector strips, a dark background 3½in x 13in rectangle and a lime NewStar block.
2. Join the units together. Repeat to make four of these units.

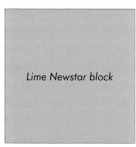

Lime Newstar block

Quilt Side Assembly Diagram

ASSEMBLE THE QUILT

1. Referring to the Quilt Layout Diagram, rotate the four quilt corners and the four quilt side units and lay them out with the remaining pink NewStar block in three rows.

2. Join the units in each row together, then join the rows, carefully matching seams.
3. Join the 4½in strips of dark background fabric end to end to make one long strip. Referring to Adding Borders in Quilting Basics, page 89, measure the length of the quilt. Cut two strips this length from the long strip. Pin, then sew them to the left and right edges of the quilt. Press seams towards the border.
4. In the same manner, measure the width of the quilt and cut two strips this length from the remaining long strip. Pin, then sew them to the top and bottom edges of the quilt. Press seams towards the border.

FINISH THE QUILT

1. Cut the length of backing fabric in half. Remove the selvages. Referring to Piecing the Backing in Quilting Basics, page 89, join the two sections together, then trim to 70in square for the backing of the quilt.
2. Referring to Preparing the Quilt Sandwich in Quilting Basics, page 89, layer the backing, batting and quilt ready for quilting.
3. Quilt as desired. *NewStar on the Block* was quilted by Rhonda Coates. On the background fabric and the NewStar blocks, she worked a free motion spiral pattern. The Nine-patch blocks were crosshatched in lime or pink thread to match the hand dyed fabrics.
4. Join the seven strips cut for the binding on the diagonal to make one long strip. Use it to bind the quilt, referring to Binding the Quilt in Quilting Basics, page 89.

Quilt Layout Diagram

Gretchen's Makeover

THIS QUILT WAS INSPIRED by Kaye England's technique for making the Gretchen block. Usually this block is made in soft muted tones or plaids but I decided that it was time that this very traditional block had a complete makeover. Bright hand dyed colors and machine embroidery give it a very contemporary look and bring it into the 21st century. The plain border is a great place for some appliqué, embroidery or quilting, with the outer border showcasing the commercial print used as a background in the blocks.

MATERIALS
12 hand dyed fat eighths [9in x 21in (25cm x 55cm)] – two shades of six different colors: light green, dark green, light blue, dark blue, light purple, dark purple, light pink, dark pink, light orange, dark orange, light yellow and dark yellow (blocks)
1¾yd (1.6m) multicolor spot commercial print fabric (blocks and borders)
1yd (90cm) plain or tone-on-tone black commercial print fabric
2⅞yd (2.6m) backing fabric
Batting at least 51in x 63in (129cm x 159cm)
Neutral sewing thread
Monofilament thread (quilting)
Black and variegated rayon thread (machine embroidery)
Sewing machine
General sewing supplies
Pfaff Card 354 for embroidery (optional)

CUT THE FABRIC
From each of the 12 hand dyed fabrics, cut:
• Four squares, 4⅞in
• Four squares, 2⅞in
From the multicolor spot commercial print fabric, cut:
• Five strips, 2½in x width of fabric (Border 3)
• Three strips, 1in x width of fabric (Borders 1 and 2)
• Six strips, 4⅞in x width of fabric. Cross cut into 48 squares, 4⅞in.
• Five strips, 2¼in x width of fabric (binding)
From the black fabric, cut:
• Three strips, 7in x width of fabric (Border 2)
• Four strips, 2⅞in x width of fabric. Cross cut into 48 squares, 2⅞in.

MAKE THE BLOCKS
Don't worry about where to place each color – it is too time consuming. Match the two small hand dyed triangles in each block; other than that concentrate on variety so that when the blocks are joined the pinwheels that form have four different colors in them.

Intermediate

Designed and made by Gail Simpson; inspired by a workshop with Kaye England
Finished size: 47in x 59in (119.5cm x 150cm)
Finished block size: 12in square

1. Mark a diagonal line on the back of each of the large 48 hand dyed squares. Match each square with a multicolor spot square.

2. Stitch a scant ¼in on either side of the drawn line. Cut along the line.

3. Finger press the pieced squares open with the seam allowances towards the multicolor spot triangle. Make 96 pieced squares. Trim the corner ears.

4. Separate the pieced squares into two stacks, right side up. Each stack should have two pieced squares of each hand dyed color. All the squares in each stack should be orientated the same way.

5. Cut each of the 2⅞in hand dyed fabric squares in half diagonally. As you cut, put the triangles in two stacks, right side up. Keep the triangles in each stack in the same order. When you have cut all the squares, place the stacks next to one of the stacks of pieced squares, as shown in Diagram 1.

6. Cut each of the 2⅞in black squares in half diagonally. Put them right side up in two equal stacks, and place the stacks next to the other stack of pieced squares, as shown in Diagram 1.

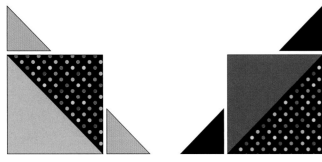

Diagram 1

7. Double check that your stacks of pieced squares and triangles match the diagram: the stacks of small hand dyed triangles should be adjacent to a large multicolor spot triangle; the stacks of small black triangles should be adjacent to a large hand dyed fabric triangle.

8. Flip the small triangles over onto the pieced squares, right sides together. Sew them in place (see Diagram 2). Press the seam allowance toward the small triangle.

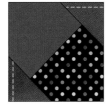

Diagram 2

9. Flip a unit with small black triangles on to a unit with small hand dyed triangles, right sides together. Trim the pieced squares so that they are even with the edges of the two small triangles (see Diagram 3).

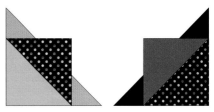
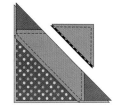

Diagram 3

10. Sew the two units together along the newly cut edge, with a ¼in seam. Finger press the seam allowance open to even out the bulk. Repeat with all the units in each stack to make 48 quarter blocks (see diagram).

Quarter blocks – make 48

11. Sew four quarter blocks together to make a Gretchen block. Repeat to make 12 Gretchen blocks.

12. Lay out the Gretchen blocks in four rows of three blocks each. Join the blocks in each row together, then join the rows, carefully matching seams.

Gretchen block – make 12

ADD BORDER 1

1. This border is added to the right edge and the bottom edge of the quilt only. Sew the three 1in strips of multicolor spot fabric end to end to make one long strip. Referring to Adding Borders in Quilt Basics, page 89, measure the length of the quilt. Cut a strip this length from the long strip and sew it to the right edge of the quilt.

2. In the same manner, measure the width of the quilt and trim the remains of the long multicolor strip to this length. Sew it to the bottom edge of the quilt.

ADD BORDER 2

1. This border is also added to the right edge and the bottom edge of the quilt only. Sew the three 7in black Border 2 strips end to end to make one long strip. Cut it into one square, 7in for the corner and two strips, one a little longer than the quilt and one a little wider than the quilt.

2. From the remaining 1in multicolor spot strip left over from Border 1, cut two 7in lengths. Sew them to one end of each of the black Border 2 strips.

3. Embroider or appliqué the Border 2 strips and the 7in square cut for the corner as desired. Bear in mind that the strips will be trimmed, so keep well away from the raw edges. The border of *Gretchen's Makeover* was machine embroidered: Gail designed a positive/negative thread version of a quarter block from the quilt and then digitized it. After all of the separate block motifs were embroidered, a meandering machine chain stitch was used to string them together. The embroidery was worked in a bright variegated rayon thread. The corner block was embroidered using Pfaff Card 354 – Fine Line Art, design 5.

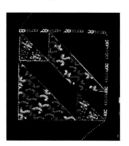
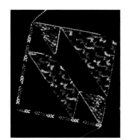

4. Referring to Adding Borders in Quilting Basics, page 89, measure the quilt horizontally and vertically, and trim the embellished Border 2 strips to 6½in wide x required length. Trim from the end of the strip without the multicolored strip on it. Trim the corner block to 6½in square.

5. Pin, then sew the longer Border 2 strip to the right edge of the quilt, with the multicolored strip adjacent to the bottom edge of the quilt.

6. Join the corner block to the end of the remaining Border 2 strip that has the multicolored strip. Pin, then sew the border strip to the bottom edge of the quilt. Press the seams towards the border.

ADD BORDER 3

1. Join the 2½in strips of multicolor spot print end to end to make one long strip. Referring to Adding Borders in Quilting Basics, page 89, measure the quilt vertically. Cut two strips this length from the long strip. Sew them to the left and right edges of the quilt.

2. In the same manner, measure the quilt horizontally. Cut two strips this length from the long strip. Sew them to the top and bottom edges of the quilt.

FINISH THE QUILT

1. Cut the length of backing fabric in half. Remove the selvages. Referring to Making the Backing in Quilting Basics, page 89, join the two sections, then trim to 51in x 63in for the backing of the quilt.

2. Referring to Preparing the Quilt Sandwich in Quilting Basics, page 89, layer the backing, batting and quilt ready for quilting.

3. Quilt as desired. *Gretchen's Makeover* was machine quilted by Gail. After ditch stitching with monofilament thread, hooped machine embroideries from Pfaff card 354, Fine Line Art were scattered around the outer edge of the blocks with a large meander in the center. All the borders were stitched freehand with a smaller meander as a fill-in to create texture.

4. Join the five strips cut for the binding end to end to make one long strip. Use it to bind the quilt, referring to Binding the Quilt in Quilting Basics, page 89.

Fandango

THIS QUILT IS FAST, FUN AND EASY TO MAKE.
You can change the coloring and rotation to create great variations on the quilt shown. Whilst there is a lot of cutting in this quilt, the sewing is speedy, with color placement the key to the design. Choose your favorite light and dark hand dyed fabrics and just one coordinating print fabric with an overall design to give movement to this unusual fan quilt.

MATERIALS
⅜yd (30cm) each of 12 hand dyed fabrics – six light and six dark. The colors used in *Fandango* were: purple, pink, orange, yellow, green and blue.
1¾yd (1.5m) commercial print fabric (blocks, sashing, border and binding)
2¾yd (2.5m) backing fabric
Batting at least 51in (130cm) square
Neutral thread for piecing
Sewing machine
General sewing supplies
Note: The blocks in this quilt were made using traditional methods and the templates are provided. For those who prefer foundation piecing, a foundation piecing diagram is also included, although detailed instructions for this technique are not provided.

CUT THE FABRIC
From the commercial print fabric, cut:
• Four strips, 4½in x **length** of the fabric (border)
• Four strips, 2¼in x **length** of fabric (binding)
• Two strips, 2½in x **length** of fabric. Cross cut into four strips, 2½in x 21in (sashing).
• One strip, 3½in x **length** of fabric. Cross cut into 16 squares, 3½in. Then cross cut each square once on the diagonal to yield 32 half-square triangles (D) or alternatively, use the template to cut 32 Template D (blocks).
Note: When using hand dyed fabrics, reversing the templates is not necessary to create mirror images of shapes, as the fabric is the same on both sides. Once the shape has been cut out, it can be turned over when the instructions require Template B-reversed or Template C-reversed. If you ever decide to make this quilt using only commercial print fabrics, cut half of the B and C patches with the templates reversed.
From each of the light and dark purple hand dyed fabrics, cut:
• Six Template A
From each of the light and dark pink hand dyed fabrics, cut:
• Eight Template A
• Four Template B
From each of the light and dark orange hand dyed fabrics, cut:
• Four Template A
• Eight Template B
• Eight Template C
From each of the light and dark yellow hand dyed fabrics, cut:
• Four Template B
• Eight Template C
• Two squares, 3½in. Cross cut the squares once on the diagonal to yield four half-square triangles (E) or alternatively, use the template to cut four Template E.

Intermediate

Deisgned and made by Gail Simpson; quilted by Kim Bradley
Finished size: 46½in x 46½in (118.5cm x 118.5cm)
Finished block size: 6in

From each of the light and dark green hand dyed fabrics, cut:
• Eight Template B
• 16 Template C
From the light blue hand dyed fabric, cut:
• 12 Template B
• Four Template C
From the dark blue hand dyed fabric cut:
• One square, 2½in (sashing strip)
• 12 Template B
• Four Template C

MAKE THE BLOCKS

1. Referring to the diagrams, lay out the patches for the blocks. You will be making
Block 1: 4 dark, 4 light
Block 2: 2 dark, 2 light
Block 3: 2 dark, 2 light
Block 4: 2 dark, 2 light
Block 5: 4 dark, 4 light
Block 6: 4 dark, 4 light

Block 1

Block 2

Block 3

Block 4

Block 5

Block 6

2. For each block, join a B patch to one side of A, and a B-reversed patch to the other. See Diagram 1.

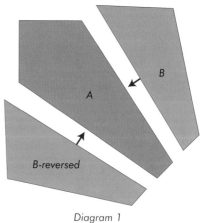

Diagram 1

3. Then join a C patch to the B patch and a C-reversed to the B-reversed patch. See Diagram 2.

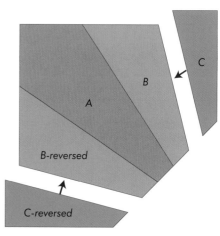

Diagram 2

4. Gently press all seams towards the A patch, being careful not to stretch the bias edges.
5. Join a yellow E triangle to the base of each Block 2. See Diagram 3.

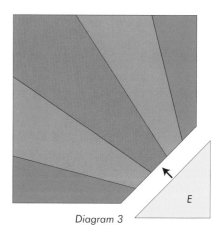

Diagram 3

6. Join a print fabric D triangle to the base of all the remaining blocks. Press seam allowance towards the D triangles. If you cut

your D and E triangles from a 3½in square, they will be slightly too large. See Diagram 4. Trim the sides of the triangle so that they are even with the edge of the block.

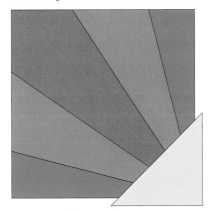

Diagram 4

7. Repeat these steps to make a total of 36 blocks.

ASSEMBLE THE QUILT

1. Join the blocks into four large units. To do this, start by laying out the blocks in three rows of three:
Row 1: Block 1, Block 4, Block 5
Row 2: Block 3, Block 1, Block 6
Row 3: Block 5, Block 6, Block 2
See Diagram 5.

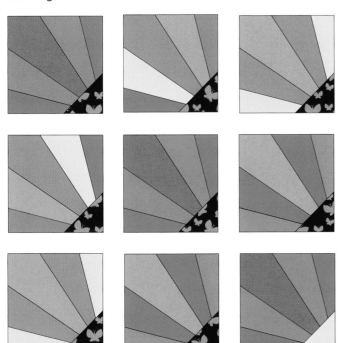

Diagram 5

2. Sew the blocks in each row together, then sew the rows together, carefully matching seams. Repeat to make two units from light blocks and two units from dark blocks.
3. Refer to the photo of the quilt to lay out the units in two rows of two with the correct orientation. Each unit should measure 18½in square, but it doesn't matter if yours differs slightly from this.

4. Measure the units – if they are different from each other, calculate their average length. Trim the 2½in strips cut from printed fabric to this length. Place them between the units – two will be vertical and two will be horizontal. Stitch the vertical sashing strips between the units in each row. Press seams towards the sashing strips.
5. Join the remaining sashing strips to the 2½in dark blue hand-dyed square. Join this strip between the two rows of sashed units, carefully aligning the blocks and the small center square.

ADD THE BORDER

1. Referring to Adding Borders in Quilting Basics, page 89, trim to size, pin, then sew two of the 4½in strips of print fabric to the left and right edges of the quilt. Press the seam allowances towards the border strips.
2. In the same manner, add the two 4½in border strips to the top and bottom edges of the quilt. See Diagram 6. Press seam allowances towards the border strips.

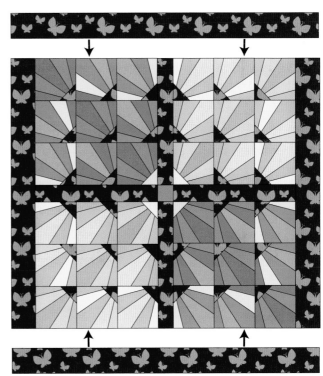

Diagram 6

FINISH THE QUILT

1. Cut the length of backing fabric in half. Remove the selvages. Referring to Piecing the Backing in Quilting Basics, page 89, join the two sections together, then trim to 49½in square for the backing of the quilt.
2. Referring to Preparing the Quilt Sandwich in Quilting Basics, page 89, layer the backing, batting and quilt ready for quilting.
3. Quilt as desired. *Fandango* was machine quilted by Kim Bradley. She worked Baptist Fans over the entire surface of the quilt.
4. Join the four strips cut for the binding end to end to make one long strip. Use it to bind the quilt, referring to Binding the Quilt in Quilting Basics, page 89.

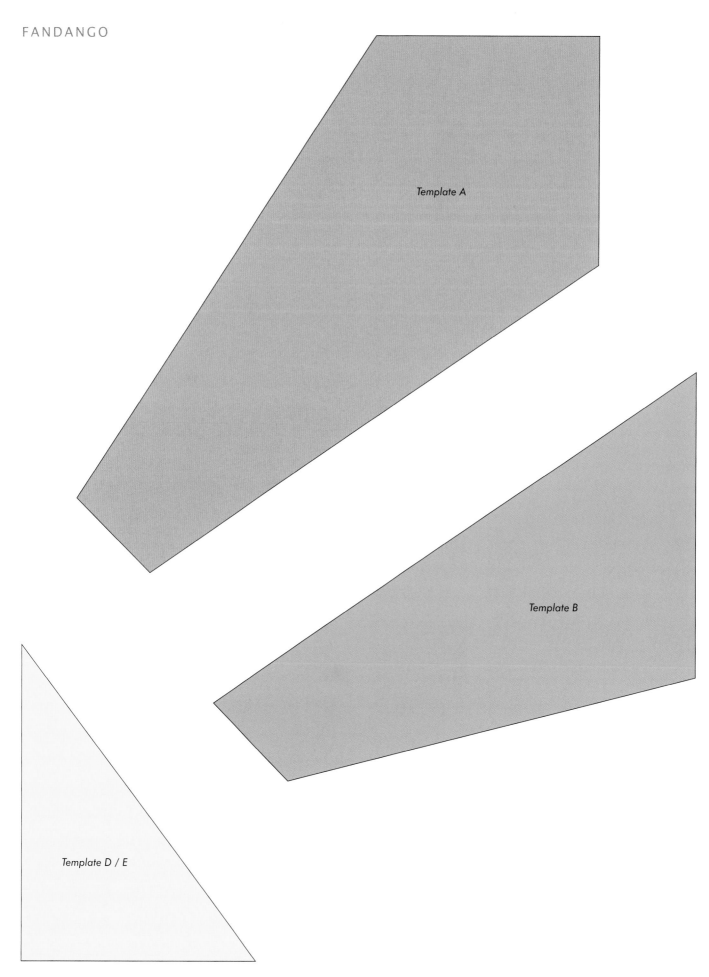

Template A

Template B

Template D / E

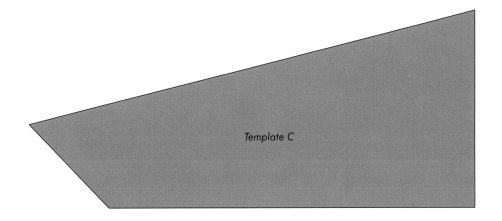

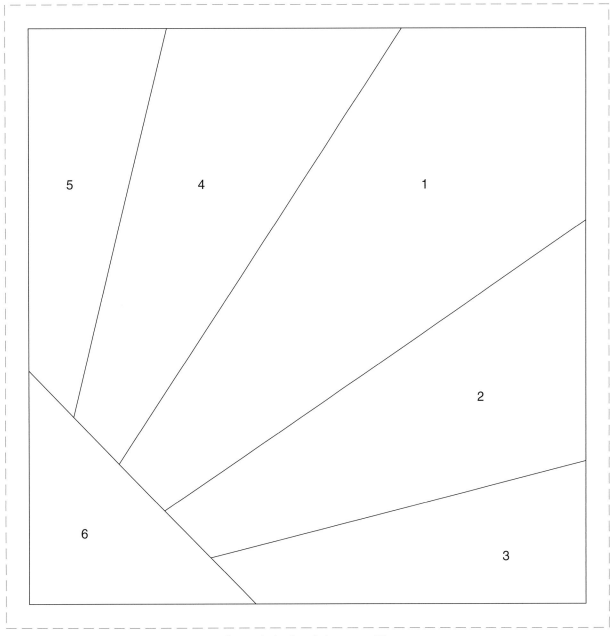

Paper piecing foundation – trace 36

RailStar

WHEN I FOUND A BEAUTIFUL DARK PRINT with shades of green, purple and brown with subtle movement, I knew it needed only a few bright colors and simple piecing to make it glow! I chose a clear rainbow palette of just six colors – gold, orange, pink, purple, blue and green. The design is a variation of Post and Rail, with a break through the center for the pieced stars. These could be replaced with appliqué and/or embroidery if you prefer.

MATERIALS

6 hand dyed fat quarters. In *RailStar*, gold, green, orange, pink, purple and blue were used.
3yd (2.7m) dark commercial print fabric
3¼yd (3m) backing fabric
58in x 70in (145cm x 175cm) batting
Rotary cutter, ruler and mat
Neutral sewing thread
Sewing machine and general sewing supplies

CUT THE FABRIC

From the gold hand dyed fabric, cut:
• Three strips, 2½in x 21in (blocks)
• One rectangle, 2½in x 14½in (blocks)
From the green hand dyed fabric, cut:
• Two strips, 2½in x 21in (blocks)
• One rectangle, 2½in x 7½in (blocks)
From the orange hand dyed fabric, cut:
• Five strips, 2½in x 21in (blocks)
From the pink hand dyed fabric, cut:
• Six strips, 2½in x 21in (blocks)
• One rectangle, 2½in x 7½in (blocks)
From the purple hand dyed fabric, cut:
• Three strips, 2½in x 21in (blocks)
• One rectangle, 2½in x 14½in (blocks)
From the blue hand dyed fabric, cut:
• Six strips 2½in x 21in. Cross cut the strips to yield 48 squares, 2½in (star points).
• Seven squares, 3½in (star centers)
Set the remaining pieces of the hand dyed fabrics aside for Border 2.
From the dark commercial print fabric, cut:
• 11 strips, 1½in x width of fabric (blocks)
• Three strips, 3½in x width of fabric. Cross cut the strips to yield 30 squares, 3½in (stars and Border 1 corners).
• Six strips, 3½in x width of fabric. Cross cut the strips to yield 20 rectangles, 3½in x 6½in (A), two rectangles, 3½in x 9½in (B), and six rectangles, 3½in x 12½in (C).
• Four strips, 3½in x width of fabric (Border 1)
• Six strips, 3½in x width of fabric (Border 3)
• Seven strips, 2¼in x width of fabric (binding)

Designed and made by Gail Simpson; quilted by Nicole Bridges
Finished size: 54in x 66in (137cm x 168cm)

MAKE THE POST AND RAIL BLOCKS

1. Sew each 2½in strip cut from the green, gold, orange, pink and purple hand dyed fabrics to a 1½in strip of dark commercial print fabric. (Do not use any of the blue hand dyed strips at this stage.) Because the hand dyed strips are shorter than the commercial print strips, you will be able to sew two or more hand dyed strips to each commercial print strip. Press the seam allowances towards the commercial print fabric. Your strip sets should measure 3½in wide.

2. Cross cut each strip set into 3½in squares, as shown in Diagram 1. The number of pieced squares featuring each of the hand dyed fabrics in this project is:

- green: 14
- gold: 22
- orange: 30
- pink: 38
- purple: 22

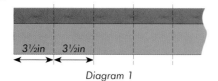

3½in   3½in

Diagram 1

MAKE THE STAR POINTS

1. The points for the star blocks are made using the connector method first developed and published by Mary Ellen Hopkins. Referring to Connectors in Quilting Basics, page 89, make 20

Double star point patches – make 20

Single star point patches – make 8

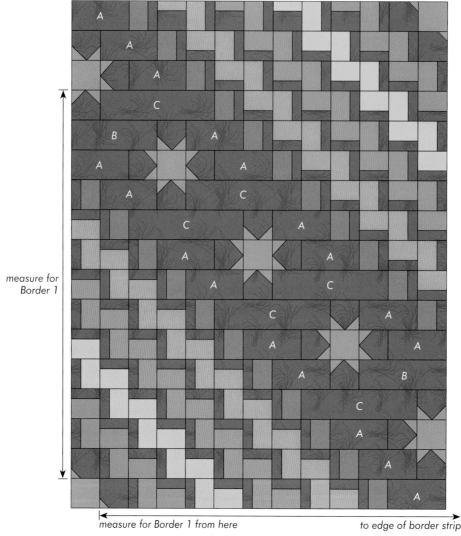

measure for Border 1

measure for Border 1 from here   to edge of border strip

Quilt Center Layout Diagram

double star point patches, and eight single star point patches using the 2½in squares of blue hand dyed fabric and the 3½in squares of dark commercial print fabrics. (You will use the remaining 2½in squares of blue hand dyed fabrics when assembling the quilt.)

ASSEMBLE THE QUILT CENTER

1. Referring to the Quilt Center Layout Diagram, lay out the Post and Rail blocks, the A, B and C strips of dark commercial print fabric, squares of blue hand dyed fabric (center of star blocks) and the connector units in 17 rows.
2. Double check the orientation of each Post and Rail block and their position in the layout to ensure that you create a zigzag pattern with these blocks.
3. Join the units in each row together. When all 17 rows have been sewn, join the rows together, carefully matching seams. Four stars are incomplete – they will be finished when you add Border 1.

ADD BORDER 1

1. The Border 1 strips for the left and right edges of the quilt are exactly the same. Measure the length of your quilt from the bottom edge of one blue hand dyed square to the top edge of the other on each of the left and right sides of the quilt center, as indicated on the Quilt Center Layout Diagram. In theory the distance should be 39in, but if you follow these steps it doesn't matter what the measurement actually is.
2. Trim two of the strips of dark commercial print fabric cut for Border 1 to this length + ½in.
3. Referring to Diagram 2, sew the units indicated to each end of these strips. Then sew the strips to the left and right edges of the quilt, carefully matching seams so that the star points are aligned with the relevant star centers.
4. The Border 1 strips for the top and bottom edges of the quilt are exactly the same. Measure the width of your quilt from the inner edge of one blue hand dyed square to the edge of the quilt, as indicated on the Quilt Center Layout Diagram. In

Diagram 2

theory, the distance should be 39½in, but it doesn't matter if your quilt is slightly different.
5. Trim the remaining two dark commercial print fabric strips cut for Border 1 to this length + ½in.
6. Referring to Diagram 3, sew a single star point connector unit and one dark commercial print 3in square to one end of the strip. Then sew the strips to the top and bottom edges of the quilt, carefully matching seams so that the star blocks are completed.

Diagram 3

ADD BORDERS 2 AND 3

1. From the remaining pieces of hand dyed fabric, cut strips 1½in wide and of various lengths. You will need sufficient strips so that when they are joined end to end they total at least 220in.

2. Join the strips end to end using diagonal seams.
3. Referring to Adding Borders in Quilting Basics, page 89, measure the length of the quilt. Cut two strips this length from the long multicolored strip and stitch them to the left and right edges of the quilt.
4. Measure the width of the quilt. Cut two strips this length from the long multicolored strip and stitch them to the top and bottom edges. Note that in *Railstar*, these strips were cut so that when sewn to the quilt, the colors at the ends of the top and bottom border strips matched those at the ends of the left and right border strips, creating the illusion that the fabric wrapped around the corners of the quilt center.
5. Join the 3½in strips of dark commercial print fabric cut for Border 3 end to end to make one long strip. Referring to Adding Borders in Quilting Basics, page 89, repeat steps 3 and 4 to add Border 3 to the quilt.

FINISH THE QUILT

1. Cut the length of backing fabric in half. Remove the selvages. Referring to Piecing the Backing in Quilting Basics, page 89, join the two sections and trim to 58in x 70in for the backing of the quilt.
2. Referring to Preparing the Quilt Sandwich in Quilting Basics, page 89, layer the backing, batting and quilt ready for quilting.
3. Quilt as desired. *RailStar* was machine quilted by Nicole Bridges in an overall swirling design on the diagonal using multicolored thread.
4. Join the six strips cut for the binding to make one long strip. Use it to bind the quilt, referring to Binding the Quilt in Quilting Basics, page 89.

Gallery

Topsy Turvy Dragonflies
Designed by Gail Simpson
Patchwork and quilting by Rhonda Coates
Once you've made the units for a Topsy Turvy quilt, experiment with their layout. Here Rhonda used her units
and two commercial print fabrics – one featuring multicolored dragonflies – to piece a square lap quilt.

Chained Windmills
Designed and made by
Gail Simpson; quilted by Kaye Brown
This quilt combines two traditional
patchwork blocks, a glorious array
of hand dyed fabrics – including
a multicolored one for the blades
of the Windmill blocks – and two
commercial print fabrics.

Chained Windmills
Designed by Gail Simpson
Patchwork by Fay Winther; quilting by Rhonda Coates
A different array of hand dyed fabrics combine with two
deep dark commercial print fabrics and some glorious
quilting to make another fabulous Windmill quilt.

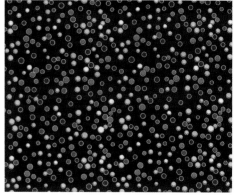

Whirlygigs
Designed and made by Gail Simpson;
quilted by Nicole Bridges
Another traditional block turned into
something quite contemporary in look with
the use of hand dyed fabrics and a fun
multicolored spot background fabric.

Whirlygigs
Designed by Gail Simpson
Patchwork and quilting by Fay Winther
Autumn toned commercial prints and a
very light background fabric create a very
different backdrop for these hand dyed fabrics.
A much more formal quilt, enhanced by richly
detailed quilting.

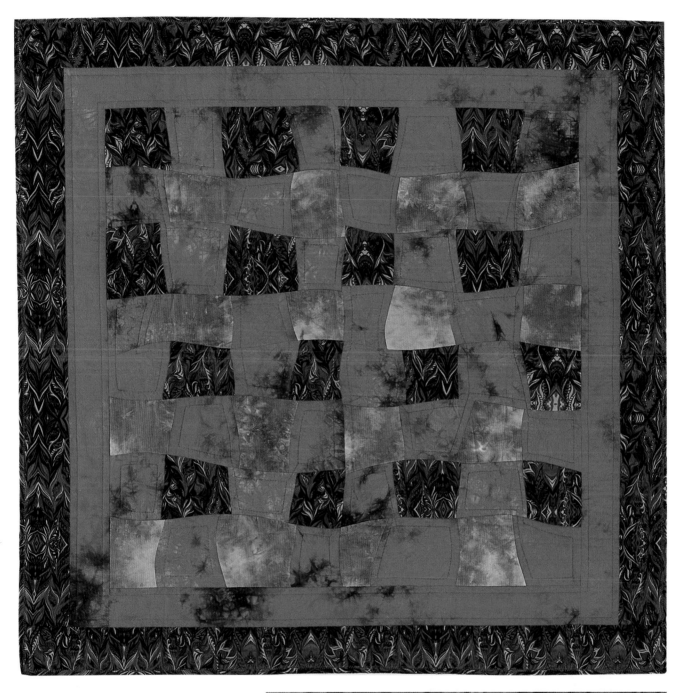

Scarlet
Designed and made by Gail Simpson
A fun quilt where the hand dyed fabrics really
steal the show.

In a Spin
Designed and made by Gail Simpson
This wholecloth quilt was inspired by a Kaye England workshop. Hand dyed fabrics complement
a busy multicolor floral, a bold stripe and some tone-on-tone striped commercial print fabrics.

Desert Sunset Tablerunner
Designed and made by Gail Simpson
Another example of hand dyed fabrics used in traditional patchwork blocks to yield a piece unexpectedly subtle and sophisticated.

Triple the Fun
Designed and made by Gail Simpson
Wow! This quilt is loads of fun. The large novelty commercial print does all sorts of surprising things when cut into small wedges, and its colors really 'pop' thanks to a glorious selection of hand dyed fabrics.

Kimono Trio
Designed and made by Gail Simpson
These three pieces have a Japanese theme, dictated by the main commercial print. The hand dyed fabrics reflect the mellow apricot and grey-blue tones within this print; the complementary grey print brings a calming influence, whilst the other hand dyed colors take it from bland to colorful.

Quilting Basics

These instructions are not a beginner's guide to everything you need to know to make a quilt. Rather, they are some hints and tips that will help explain specific steps that I have used in the instructions for projects in this book, along with some insights into the work methods that I use when making my own quilts. I've been sewing for more than 50 years, and making quilts for the past 13 years. My methods, therefore, have been truly tried and tested!

As a general guide, use the best quality fabric and tools that you can afford; strive for the highest level of accuracy in your sewing that you can achieve; and relax and enjoy the process of creating your own masterpiece.

FABRIC SELECTION

- I love the variety of commercial prints available. No, you will not see many little floral prints in my work, but I love them just the same. They just don't fit in with what I do. Brights, stripes, prints with both light and dark backgrounds and, last but not least, the occasional ugly, will all be found in my fabric stash. I have steered away from stark plain black backgrounds as I find these stereotype the use of hand dyed fabrics.

- Where do I start when choosing fabrics? That is a hard question to answer – sometimes I see a commercial print and know one day I will find a way to use it; other times inspiration comes from a new color set of hand dyed fabrics. Take *For the Print* as an example. I fell instantly in love with the Alexander Henry print fabric I used in that quilt, although it sat in my stash for two years, waiting for inspiration to strike. The only thing I knew from the very beginning was that it needed to be the feature of the quilt, used with simple piecing.

The commercial print featured in For the Print

The background used in *RailStar* was one of those hard to find prints with surprising deep, dark hollows and brighter purple and green highlights. Okay, so the purple band of blocks towards the center of the quilt may get a little lost, but the

The commercial print featured in Railstar

background becomes more important there and the blue stars just float out to greet you. *Almost Country* has a great background fabric with tiny bars of just two or three colors from the hand dyed fabrics I chose to work with. The turkey feathers commercial print used in the border pulled the whole thing together.

The background and border prints used in Almost Country.

- My concept is to keep the piecing simple and make the fabrics do the work. As a result, I am always on the lookout for unusual prints. Much to my delight I have found that a lot of my fabric choices are relegated to the 'hard to use' category and wind up in the 'specials' at the quilt shops!

PREPARING FABRICS

- It is advisable to use 100% cotton fabric, particularly if the item is to be laundered. Cotton fabrics are light weight, easy to sew, durable and readily washed.

'Hard to use' fabrics teamed with an array of hand dyed can result in fabulous quilts.

- The yardage listed in the Materials list for each project is based on fabrics that are 44in wide. To allow for some shrinkage and wastage when cutting, I have calculated the cutting instructions on having a 42in usable width of fabric. Furthermore, the yardage shown is the amount of fabric that I recommend you buy if you are purchasing fabric especially for your project. It includes about 4in (10cm) additional fabric so that you won't run out if the fabric is cut crookedly at the store or if you need to trim to straighten the edge of the fabric as you make multiple cuts. If, however, you have some fabrics in your stash that are just a little less than those shown in the Materials list, you may find that you have enough for a project.

- I like to give the customers of Cotton Patch Fabrics good value. I cut fabric for my packets and medleys of hand dyes so that fat eighths are 10in wide, not the American standard 9in, and fat quarters are 21in wide, not the American standard 18in. If you are ordering Cotton Patch Fabrics to make one of the projects in this book, let me know so they I can sell you the fabric pack that represents the best value for you – providing sufficient fabric for the project without a lot of surplus.

- Most quiltmaking books recommend washing and pressing all the fabrics to be used in a quilt before commencing. I think this is quite a personal choice: I do not pre-wash commercial prints and my Cotton Patch hand dyed fabrics are all pre-washed during the dyeing process. They are all colorfast, having been thoroughly washed in very hot water, with a white cloth test piece. If this piece is not white at the finish, another hot wash is done.

To test any fabric for colorfastness, simply dampen it, then iron it dry on a white cloth. Any color on the white cloth indicates some excess dye in the fabric. Be very careful with glue sticks, erasable pens and spray starches – some contain a chemical that may cause bleeding, not only with hand dyeds but also commercial fabrics.

PRESSING

- I am not a big fan of pressing each and every seam in traditional patchwork with an iron. This is especially true for units made from half-square triangles, which have bias seams. I do a lot of finger pressing. I generally use an iron for pressing only after a block or section is complete.
- Also, there are some circumstances where I will finger press the seams open rather than to one side. In *Birds and Bouquet Fantasy*, for example, a number of seams meet at the top of the 'cone'. I pressed these seams open to distribute their bulk.

When a number of seams meet, such as in this block from Birds and Bouquet Fantasy, *press seams open rather than to one side, to distribute their bulk.*

- When working with curves it is a different story. Refer to the Freehand Curve Techniques section on the following pages.

ROTARY CUTTING

- Most, if not all, straight-edged geometric shapes – squares, triangles, rectangles, etc – can be cut quickly and accurately from strips of fabric using a rotary cutter, mat and ruler.

- In recent times, I've become an enthusiastic user of specialty rulers for cutting half- and quarter-squares triangles, half rectangles, bias rectangles and fan blades. The benefit of using specialist rulers is that you don't need to cut strips to awkward measurements. I strongly recommend the Nifty Notions range of rulers, which are well made, clearly marked and come with easy-to-understand instructions. I have found my cutting accuracy has improved greatly since making the change to these rulers.

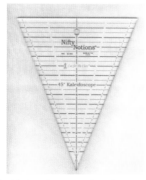

Nifty Notions have produced a range of specialist rulers, including this one, designed especially for making kaleidoscope blocks. However, I also used it for the triangles in Not Quite 1000 Pyramids.

ACCURACY IN BOTH CUTTING AND PIECING

- The most important factor in successfully making a quilt is accuracy in both cutting and piecing. A ¼in seam allowance is used throughout this book and is included in all rotary cutting instructions, with the exception of *For the Print*, which uses freehand curved piecing.
- You can improve accuracy in cutting by regularly cleaning your rotary cutter, changing the blade and ensuring the blade is not too tight. This can be tested on your mat: you should be able to roll the cutter smoothly without a lot of pressure.
- When cutting, remember 'checking twice and cutting once' is better than checking once and cutting twice!
- I'd also like to put on the record that I never, ever do all the cutting for a quilt when I first begin. I find it much less confusing to cut the patches for each part of the quilt as I need them. The instructions in this book are presented with all the cutting instructions grouped together at the beginning. It's been

done this way because that has become the industry standard, and, I admit, it does help to understand how each particular fabric will be cut and used in the quilt. Nevertheless, I stand by my recommendation that you should work your way through each project cutting the patches as you need them.

- Three things that will immediately improve your piecing are:

1. a new needle for each project
Needles do not stay sharp forever and a blunt needle will affect accuracy. I always use a size 90 (14) 'sharp' needle for piecing, as it has the piercing capacity to penetrate multiple layers of cotton fabric and stitch over seams.

2. a straight stitch needle plate
Many of today's machines come with a wide hole needle plate to accommodate decorative stitching, but it is worth the investment to purchase a straight stitch needle plate.

3. a ¼in foot for your sewing machine
You can move the needle on many machines, but this means you cannot use a straight stitch needle plate. If you do not have a ¼in machine foot, measure and place a strip of tape on the machine bed at the ¼in position and use it as a guide for the fabric.

APPLIQUÉ WITH FUSIBLE WEB

Preparation

- Trace the appliqué shapes from the pages of the book on to the paper side of the fusible web. Use a pencil and leave ½in between shapes. Remember that the shapes in the finished quilt will be the reverse of those printed in the book. Use either a light box or hold the page of the book against a well-lit window.
- Cut around each shape about ¼in *outside* the traced line. Then carefully cut the center out of each shape about ¼in *inside* the drawn line. This will leave you with a narrow strip of fusible web near the raw edge of the shape. Not only is it a cost efficient way of using the fusible web – you can use the center cutouts to trace smaller shapes – it also means that your appliqué shapes won't be stiff.
- Lay the fusible web shapes on the wrong side of the selected fabric. Keep the shape on the straight of grain. Fuse the

web to the fabric using a dry iron on a cotton setting for about five seconds.

- Cut out the shape accurately on the pencil line. Let the fusible web cool, then carefully remove the backing paper. Position the fabric appliqué shapes on a background fabric, layering where appropriate. Fuse them in place, applying slight pressure, using steam iron (cotton setting) for approximately 10 seconds.

Sewing

- Most sewing machines have a blanket stitch or something similar to use for stitching around the raw edges of the appliqué shapes. If your machine doesn't have this stitch, a narrow zigzag stitch works just as well.
- Place a sheet of fabric stabilizer such as Stitch and Tear behind the appliqué on the wrong side of the background fabric before machine stitching. This helps prevent puckering. Check the needle plate before you start stitching. If you have a straight stitch needle plate on the machine, you will break the needle as there is nowhere for it to swing. After sewing the appliqué, gently remove the stabilizer.

Threads

- Use either rayon embroidery thread in the needle and a matching cotton or polyester thread in the bobbin, or 100% cotton embroidery thread in the needle and the bobbin. If you wish to mimic the look of hand appliqué, use monofilament thread in the needle and cotton thread in the bobbin, and select a narrow blind hemstitch.
- Choose thread colors to either match or contrast with the appliqué fabrics, depending on the look that you're after.

BASIC UNITS

Four-patch, Nine-patch, half-square triangles and quarter-square triangles are four of the basic units used in the quilts in this book.

Four-patch

- Cut two squares of light colored fabric and two squares of dark colored fabric all the same size. Lay them out as per the diagram. Join the top two squares together, then the bottom two squares. Join these two rows to form a Four-patch, matching the seams. Finger press the seams to one side.

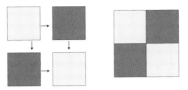

Making a Four-patch

- Each square used in a Four-patch unit can be cut from a single fabric or it can be pieced from several different fabrics. For example, you could make a Four-patch from two plain squares combined with two squares pieced from half-square triangles.

Nine-patch

- Cut four squares of light colored fabric and five squares of dark colored fabric all the same size. Lay them out as per the diagram. Join the three squares in each row together. Join the three rows to form a Nine-patch, matching the seams. Finger press the seams to one side.

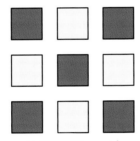

Making a Nine-patch

- Each square used in a Nine-patch unit can be cut from a single fabric or it can be pieced from several different fabrics. For example, you could make a Nine-patch from plain squares combined with squares pieced from half-square triangles.

Half-square triangles

- The math for calculating the size of the square you need to start with to create half-square triangles is "finished unit size plus $\frac{7}{8}$in". That is, for a finished 3in block, start by cutting a square 3in + $\frac{7}{8}$in = 3$\frac{7}{8}$in. Cut the square once on the diagonal to yield two half-square triangles.

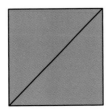

Half-square triangles are made by cutting a square once on the diagonal.

Squares made from two half-square triangles

- Cut two squares the same size from different fabrics. Draw a diagonal line on the wrong side of the lighter square. Match the squares right sides together. Stitch a $\frac{1}{4}$in either side of the drawn line.

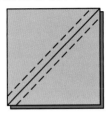

Stitch $\frac{1}{4}$in either side of the diagonal to make a square pieced from two half-square triangles.

- Cut along the line to yield two pieced squares, each made of half-square triangles. Finger press the seam allowance towards the darker fabric.

Quarter-square triangles

- The math for calculating the size of the square you need to start with to create quarter-square triangles is "finished unit size plus 1$\frac{1}{4}$in". That is, for a finished 6in block, start by cutting a square 6in + 1$\frac{1}{4}$in = 7$\frac{1}{4}$in. Cut the square on both diagonals to yield four quarter-square triangles.

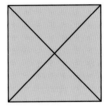

Quarter-square triangles are made by cutting a square twice on the diagonals.

Flying Geese

- The Flying Geese block is a good example of using one quarter-square and two half-square triangles. While there are a number of different ways of making Flying Geese block, I have found cutting and piecing them from triangles the most accurate.

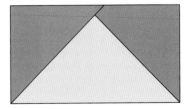

Flying Geese blocks are made from one quarter-square triangle and two half-square triangles.

CONNECTORS

- Whenever possible, I like to use the 'connector method' developed by Mary Ellen Hopkins. This method eliminates a bias seam and maintains the integrity of the fabric square, as only the middle layer of fabric is cut away. Having said that, there are occasions when I leave the middle layer in place – such as when I am stitching a light colored fabric over a dark colored fabric that will show through a single layer.
- Draw or fold a diagonal line across the connector square. Place the unfolded square on the corner of the appropriate background square, matching cut edges. Stitch along the line. Trim away the fabric, ¼in from the stitched line. Cut the connector fabric only. Do not cut the background fabric. Finger press the top layer in place towards the corner. The 'loose' top layer is subsequently caught in the seam, securing it in place.

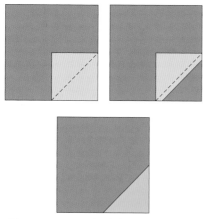

The connector method of sewing triangles

- Connectors can also be used with rectangles in lieu of squares and are made in the same manner.

FREEHAND CURVED TECHNIQUES

- Although curved seams are not all that common in traditional patchwork, I find that they add a wonderful element of whimsy and surprise to a quilt. *For the Print* uses freehand curved techniques,

so I've provided detailed instructions here that will assist you with that project. *Scarlet* shown in the Gallery section was also made used freehand curves. You can apply these techniques to other quilts to turn something that might be 'ho hum' into something stunning.

- To cut fabrics with a gentle curve, I recommend a 28mm rotary cutter. It allows better control, particularly when cutting through more than two layers, than a larger rotary cutter.
- The diagram down the center of this page is my idea of a gentle curve. A curve like this can be easily stitched with a narrower than normal seam allowance and tamed into submission with a steam iron. A ¼in seam allowance is not essential; the narrower the better and yes, the steam iron will become your best friend.
- Remember to always cut gentle curves – no S bends!
- To sew curved seams, set your stitch length at 2. You will be cutting and stitching across previously stitched seams and this shorter stitch length prevents the unraveling of seams as you push and pull them around the curves.
- If you have a needle down facility – engage it. As I sew on a Pfaff machine, I have built-in dual feed, which I also engage. If you have a similar feature on your machine, it is a good idea to use it. Generally a walking foot is too bulky and makes it difficult to align the hills and valleys for the opposing curves and stitch very narrow seams consistently.
- Use a hot iron and steam. Iron each seam as you go. I like to iron from the top, with the point of the iron pushing the seam allowance forward. If you hold the fabric up with your other hand, the seam allowance will go forward almost automatically.
- To sew curved strips together, you need opposing curves for the seam line. You achieve this by cutting through two layers of fabric, one stacked on top of the other. I don't find it necessary to mark matching points. At first you may choose to use a few pins matching the hills and valleys. As long as the strips are matched at one end, after some practice you will find it is easier to work without pins.
- To sew the strips together, make your first few stitches and stop with the needle

down. Keeping the bottom layer firm, ease the top layer around to align the raw edges. Continue in this fashion until you complete the seam.

STRAIGHT SETTING

• When blocks are set together square, edge to edge or separated by sashing strips, they are said to have been assembled in a straight setting.
• To assemble a quilt in a straight setting, lay out the blocks in horizontal rows. If you are using sashings, lay the sashing strips between the blocks.
• Stitch the blocks and sashings in each row together. Then stitch the rows together matching the seam lines at each junction. Examples of projects that have been assembled with a straight setting are *Fandango*, *Gretchen's Makeover*, *NewStar on the Block* and *Topsy Turvy*.

DIAGONAL SETTING

• A diagonal set is also sewn in rows. The difference is that the rows are diagonal and setting triangles rather than full blocks are sewn to the ends of each row. Join the rows, then finally add the corner triangles.
• How do you know what size to cut these triangles? In order to maintain the straight of grain on the outside edges of both corner and setting triangles, they are cut from squares, as follows:
• side triangles: measure your pieced block across the diagonal and add 3in. Cut a square with sides that dimension, then cut the square twice on the diagonal. This will yield four quarter-square setting triangles with the straight grain on the outside edge when pieced.
• corner triangles: add 2in to the block's finished size. Cut two squares with sides that dimension and cut each square once on the diagonal to yield four half-square corner triangles.
Note: These measurements allow for some 'float' around the quilt center after joining the rows. The 'float' can be trimmed back ¼in outside the points of the blocks for a sharp effect if desired. If you want more 'float', cut both the base squares larger.
• There are now specialty rulers available for cutting these setting triangles from strips. I prefer to use the rulers as they are more accurate and fabric efficient

than cutting large squares on the bias.
• Once all the setting and corner triangles have been cut and added to the lay out, sew the blocks together in diagonal rows and stitch a setting triangle to each end of the row. Join the diagonal rows, then add the corner triangles. The corner triangles will be a little larger than required, but this allows for trimming to square. The larger you cut both setting and corner triangles, the more your blocks will 'float'. Be careful as you stitch these triangles to the adjacent blocks as you are handling bias edges. *Fun with Nine Patch* is an example of a project that has been assembled with a diagonal setting. The center strip of Bouquet blocks in *Birds and Bouquet Fantasy* was also made this way.

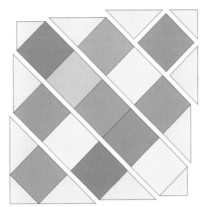

Join the blocks together in diagonal rows when assembling a quilt with a diagonal set.

ADDING BORDERS

• I have used square (non-mitered) borders for all the quilts in this book. I always sew the left and right borders in place first, then the top and bottom borders.
• To measuring the length for the borders follow these steps. Repeat them for multiple borders.
• Measure the length of the quilt down both sides and through the center. If there is a slight difference, calculate the average length. Cut the fabric for the left and right borders to the average length.
• Mark the halfway point on both the quilt and each border strip.
• Pin the border strips to the quilt, right sides together, at each end and the matching halfway points. Sew in place.
• Measure the width of the quilt at the top, bottom and through the center. If there is a slight difference, calculate the average

width. Cut the fabric for the top and bottom borders to the average length.
• Mark the halfway point on both the quilt and each border strip.
• Pin the border strips to the quilt, right sides together, at each end and the matching halfway points. Sew in place.
• Where I have used pieced, plain or embroidered blocks in the corners of the border, all borders are cut to the actual width and length of the pieced quilt top. Measure, cut, mark, pin and sew the left and right border strips in place as described above. Sew the corner blocks to each end of the top and bottom border strips. Mark, pin and sew the top and bottom borders in place, carefully matching the seams of the corner blocks with the side border seams where they meet. Press all seam allowances towards the borders.

BATTING

• This is the filling for the quilt and is available in a variety of fibers, from 100% polyester to 100% cotton or wool, plus all the mixtures in between. The type chosen will depend on whether the quilt is to be hand or machine quilted and whether the finished quilt is to be draped on a bed or hung on a wall.
• There are many variables. I have heard very good reports on the silk/wool variety now available. Most of the quilts in this book have been made with 100% cotton batting and have been washed once or twice.
• The batting should be at least two inches larger all round than the quilt top to allow for shrinkage during quilting. If you are planning to send your quilt top to a longarm quilter, you might like to increase this overhang to four inches. As so many people have their quilts quilted on longarm machines these days, the yardage in the Materials list for most of the projects in this book is based on a four inch overhang.

PIECING THE BACKING

• This will be the reverse of your masterpiece and can be just as interesting as the quilt top.
• The backing will need to be at least two inches larger all round than the quilt top to allow for shrinkage during quilting if you are quilting on a domestic sewing

machine or hand quilting. Again, allow a four inch overhang if you quilt is to be quilted on a longarm machine.

- The backing can be either pieced or plain. There are many wider fabrics available for whole piece backings. If you are working with regular 44in wide fabric, you will need either twice the length or width of the quilt, plus 10in.

- I recommend piecing the backing together with the seams as depicted in the diagrams, rather than having one seam fall across or down the middle of the quilt. To piece a backing like this following these steps:

- Snip into the top of the fabric, about a $\frac{1}{2}$in in from the edge and tear the selvage away. Repeat with the other selvage. This will not stretch the fabrics: stretching only occurs when you tear across the width of the fabric.

- Cut the length of fabric in half. Fold one piece long edges matching to find its center. Snip and tear through the length as you did in the previous step to remove the selvages. Sew a half width of fabric to each side of the full width using a $\frac{1}{4}$in seam allowance. Press the seams open.

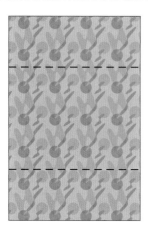

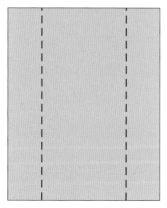

Piece the backing fabric to avoid having a seam run down or across the center of the quilt.

PREPARING THE QUILT SANDWICH

- Press both the quilt backing and top.
- Lay the backing right side down on a flat surface and secure with masking tape and/or large bulldog clips. Lay the batting on top, smoothing out any creases as you go. If using bulldog clips, secure with the backing. Lay the quilt top, right side up on top of the batting, ensuring it is centered over the backing and batting. Smooth out from the center and secure to the under layers with a few pins or the bulldog clips.
- For hand quilting, tack or baste the layers together with a large running stitch. For machine quilting, pin the layers together with spacing as required for the batting you are using.

QUILTING

- I'm not going to provide a detailed account of the quilting stitch or choosing and implementing a quilting design. There are numerous books specifically on this topic, and I recommend that you refer to one of them. My favorite is *Quilting Makes the Quilt* by Lee Cleland. I do not consider myself an expert quilter and often rely on my longarm quilting friends, particularly for larger quilts.
- To provide you with some ideas, however, I have described the quilting that has been worked on each of the projects in this book.

BINDING

- Most of my bindings are machine stitched to the back of the quilt first, then machine stitched in place on the front of the quilt using a decorative stitch. Perhaps it is a statement about breaking the rules. It is also that I dread hand stitching and I like the finish that this method gives me. I think blanket stitch works particularly well when stitching the binding to the front of the quilt where there is blanket stitch appliqué in the body of the quilt.
- I generally use a decorative thread, either cotton or rayon, with the bobbin thread matched to the color of the backing. Machine tension is slightly reduced and normally I use a size 90 needle to accommodate both the thread and the thickness of the layers.
- After quilting, my quilts are trimmed back to square. I then run a stay stitch

around their perimeter using a slightly longer than normal stitch, a little under a $\frac{1}{4}$in in from the edge. This stitching can be removed later if required, however it is normally enclosed within the binding.

- Cut sufficient 2$\frac{1}{4}$in strips for the binding: (quilt length x 2) + (quilt width x 2) + 10in-12in for seams and corners. Join the strips together with 45 degree seams and press the seams open (to distribute the bulk).

- Cut one end of the binding at a 45 degree angle. Press the binding in half lengthwise, wrong sides together, and then press under a single $\frac{1}{4}$in hem on the 45 degree angle end of the binding.

- Using a $\frac{1}{4}$in seam allowance and starting about 4in from the pressed hem, stitch the binding strip to the backing, using the previously stitched guideline for placement. Stop stitching $\frac{1}{4}$in from the corner. Remove the quilt from the machine and fold the binding strip at 45 degrees towards the top of the quilt. Then fold it down level with the next side of the guideline to create a neat corner. This will make a mitered corner when the binding is folded to the front of the quilt. Continue stitching, starting at the top of the folded strip. Repeat the process for all the other corners. Stop stitching approximately 6in from the starting point, with the needle down and the quilt remaining under the machine. Determine the length of the binding you need to enable you to insert the end inside the beginning of the binding and trim off the excess. Slip the new end into place and finish stitching the binding strip.

- Trim excess batting and backing so that they are even with the raw edge of the binding strip. Turn the folded edge over to the front of the quilt and machine stitch in place with your preferred stitch and thread.

LABEL

- Always label your quilts, before or after quilting.
- Along with the important information, like the name of the maker and the quilter and the finishing date, you may choose to include who the quilt was made for, the special occasion it commemorates, techniques that were used, or anything else that comes to mind as important to either yourself or future owners.

Gail Simpson and Cotton Patch Fabrics

Gail had been working with dyeing and painting silks for many years before teaching herself to make quilts from the few books that were then available. She then began attending patchwork classes to explore working with different fabrics and techniques. Her first forays into dyeing cotton fabrics were to satisfy her own quiltmaking needs and those of a few friends. Cotton Patch Fabrics was born.

Much to her surprise, suddenly there were not enough hours in the day to both produce the fabrics and sell them. To enable her to concentrate her efforts on dyeing, Gail elected to be a wholesaler, distributing to retail shops throughout Australia.

Gail has worked closely with her fabric supplier to source the best base cloth available. She uses a soft, even weave, quilters' muslin that stands up to her rigorous dyeing and washing procedures, whilst maintaining wonderful 'hand' in the finished product. It is fabulous for both hand and machine stitching and is compatible in weight and strength with today's commercially printed fabrics.

Initially Gail started doing the regular dark, medium and light values in various colors, and then she introduced a few fat eighths and long quarter packs to add variety to her range.

That exercise started with five or six color packs and as demand continued to rise, it became the main part of her work. There are now 22 packs of 10 colors, eight packs of 12 colors, and more than 50 colors, each in dark, medium and light values.

Amongst the packs there is something for everyone: Pastels, Dusty Pastels and Cottage Garden will be the lightest colors you will find.

Gail sees the 'hot' colors of Australian summers reflected in Candy Bright, Bold and Bright, Garden, Summer Rainbow and Summer Haze.

Or for something not quite so bright, there are packs called Autumn, Federation, Mellow Rainbow, Shadows, Mellow 1 and Mellow 2.

For the Landscape artist, there's Leaf and Litter or Sea and Sky.

Then there is the JUST range, available in pink, purple, blue, green and yellow.

And last but not least, the Just Because pack – just because Gail loved those particular colors together.

To order Gail's hand dyed fabrics, visit the Cotton Patch Fabrics' website: www.cottonpatchfabrics.com.au
International mail order is available and Gail can be contacted through her website for assistance if required.
Readers in Australia and New Zealand: check the website for your nearest retailer or contact Gail direct if you live in one of the many far flung regions with no access to retailers.

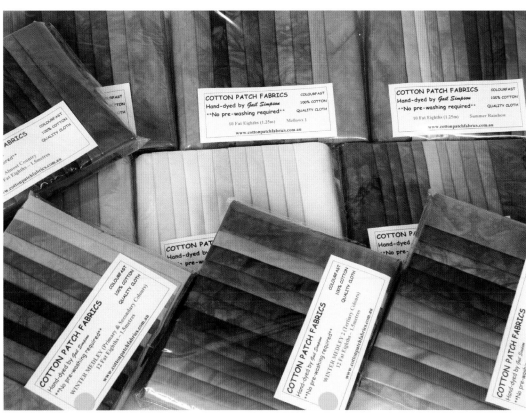